Marked by Love
Course Leaders' Guide

Practical help to Unveil the Substance of Your True Identity

Catherine Toon, MD

Publishing, LLC

MARKED BY LOVE COURSE LEADERS' GUIDE by Catherine Toon, MD
Published by Imprint Publishing
PO Box 63125 Colorado Springs, CO 80962-3125
United States

www.catherinetoon.com
Phone: (724) 677-6801
Email: info@catherinetoon.com

All rights reserved. This book or parts thereof may not be reproduced in any form, stored in a retrieval system, or transmitted in any form by any means electronic, mechanical, photocopy, recording, or otherwise without prior written permission of the publisher, except as provided by United States of America copyright law.

Copyright © 2018 by Catherine Toon
All rights reserved.

ISBN 978-0-9995910-5-5 (Paperback Edition)

Library of Congress Control Number: 2018903667

Printed in the United States of America
First Printing April 2018

Credits and Permissions:

Scripture taken from the Holy Bible, NEW INTERNATIONAL VERSION, NIV. Copyright 1973, 1978, 1984, 2011 by Biblica, Inc. Used by permission. All rights reserved worldwide.

Scripture quotations taken from the New American Standard Bible (NASB), Copyright 1960, 1962, 1963, 1968, 1971, 1972, 1973, 1975, 1977, 1995 by The Lockman Foundation. Used by permission. www.Lockman.org

Scripture quotations taken from the Amplified Bible (AMP), Copyright 2015 by The Lockman Foundation. Used by permission. www.Lockman.org

Scripture quotations taken from the Amplified Bible (AMPC), Copyright 1954, 1958, 1962, 1964, 1965, 1987 by The Lockman Foundation. Used by permission. www.Lockman.org

Scripture taken from the New King James Version. Copyright 1982 by Thomas Nelson. Used by permission. All rights reserved.

Scripture taken from The Voice. Copyright 2012 by Ecclesia Bible Society. Used by permission. All rights reserved.

Scripture taken from the King James Bible is public domain and may be used freely, without restriction and without prior permission.

Scripture quotations are taken from the Holy Bible, New Living Translation, copyright 1996, 2004, 2007, 2013, 2015 by Tyndale House Foundation. Used by permission of Tyndale House Publishers, Inc., Carol Stream, Illinois 60188. All rights reserved.

Scripture quotations marked (TLB) are taken from The Living Bible copyright 1971. Used by permission of Tyndale House Publishers, Inc., Carol Stream, Illinois 60188. All rights reserved.

Verses listed without translation references are partially quoted or inferred.

Book Cover & Photography by Granite Pillar
Editing by Becky Royer
Graphic Design by Kelsey & David Chapman

God is love. By this the love of God was in us, that God has sent His only begotten Son into the world so that we might live through Him.

1 John 4:8-9 (NASB)

Contents

Welcome Leader Letter 7

Welcome Leaders: Getting Prepared! 9

1: Introduction 29

2: The Epicenter of Universe 43

3: The Flavors of God 53

4: Who Am I? 61

5: What's Wrong? 67

6: What's Right? 73

7: The Object of God's Passion 79

8: Getting There from Here – Finishing at the Starting Point 85

9: Freaky Rest 91

10: Your Love Story 97

11: Follow Up: Your Love Story – 11th Meeting 103

A Personal Note from Catherine 107

Icebreaker Games and Activities 111

Tips for Ministering to Needier Individuals 115

Additional Resources 119

About the Author 121

Other Products by Catherine 125

Welcome Marked By Love Leader!

God is love. By this the love of God was in us, that God has sent His only begotten Son into the world so that we might live through Him.
1 John 4:8-9 (NASB)

Love is our deepest emotional and spiritual need. Without it, we shrivel up emotionally, spiritually, and physically. We limp through life. We have no idea who we really are, or ultimately, the reason we are on the planet.

I have been helping people to encounter God as Love for many years, and in doing so, have helped to restore wholeness, reveal identity and release destiny for thousands of people. And it is my mandate and *honor* to do so for you and to empower you to lead others in this! I do not believe you have this leaders' guide in your hands by accident. I believe you are being set up in the most glorious way for a serious upgrade, and to lead others to receive their upgrades.

This Leaders' Guide provides a venue for an in-depth adventurous exploration into the Person of Love and to lead others in that as well. You will not do this alone. You will do this empowered by Holy Spirit. And I will be there to help you to intimately encounter God as Love and facilitate others in their encounters.

As you do this personally and lead others in this, there will be an unveiling of the exquisite ways that you and those in your group have been created and marked by God. As you and your group connect with who you truly are, you will be empowered to make your unique mark on a world that is starving for Love!

It is *your* time to receive and *your* time to lead! I want to hear from you during your journey in receiving and leading.

It is my heart's desire that you and those you lead will be astounded by knowing Love in ways that you have never imagined, and that you would be fully flooded with Him and transformed through ongoing and regular encounters. I am so excited for you!

Love,
Catherine

WELCOME LEADERS:

GETTING PREPARED – MINDSETS
FOR AN AWESOME EXPERIENCE!

Called, Anointed, & Equipped

Calling all leaders – seasoned and just beginning!

God is all about raising people up to minister out of what they have received. If you are called, chances are, you are more equipped than you think. That calling does not have to be a huge supernatural angelic encounter, it can be a still small voice or it can be a desire in your heart. But with that, it should carry peace in your inner being, even if you are really nervous about it.

Colossians 3:15 (AMP) says:

> *Let the peace of Christ [the inner calm of one who walks daily with Him] be the controlling factor in your hearts **[deciding and settling questions that arise]**. To this peace indeed you were called as members in one body [of believers]. And be thankful [to God always].*

If you happen to desire it, but *don't* have peace in your inner man/woman, it may be that this is something that the Lord wants you to do, but desires to prepare you in some way first. Perhaps you have a tendency to try to get your identity from what you do, including serving Him. This was my story. Being delivered from that is SO freeing. However, if He is asking you to step out and you are afraid, step out by all means. You will be exhilarated with how He will move through YOU!

God's Word says, freely you have been received, now freely give (Matthew 10:8b).

When God calls you to lead others, He is also wanting to pour into you. Many times, as you help others navigate material, you will receive tremendous wisdom and revelation for yourself. As you step out to lead others, recognize that you are the student first, Holy Spirit is your Guide and Teacher, and He will equip you to guide and teach others. He is masterful at this, so you don't need to look at yourself. If He called you, He will equip and back you up!

You don't need to have all the answers. Just be authentic and honest. Let us know if you have hit a snag. But most likely, you will be amazed at how things really work out and what Holy Spirit will do through you!

Luke 12:12 (AMP) says:

For the Holy Spirit will teach you in that very hour what you ought to say.

John 14:26 (AMP) adds:

But the Helper (Comforter, Advocate, Intercessor – Counselor, Strengthener, Standby), the Holy Spirit, whom the Father will send in My name [in My place, to represent Me and act on My behalf], He will teach you all things. And He will help you remember everything that I have told you.

John 2:20 (AMP) says:

But you have an anointing from the Holy One [you have been set apart, specially gifted and prepared by the Holy Spirit], and all of you know [the truth because He teaches us, illuminates our minds, and guards us from error].

1 John 2:27b (AMP) also says:

But just as His anointing teaches you [giving you insight through the presence of the Holy Spirit] about all things, and is true and is not a lie, and just as His anointing has taught you, you must remain in Him [being rooted in Him, knit to Him].

Keep in mind, you are not responsible:

- to have all the answers
- to have it all together (Who does? I certainly don't!)

It is refreshing for people to know that you are a person with frailties and in process, depending on Holy Spirit to manifest you in fullness as a beloved son/daughter. Authenticity and personal growth are a wonderful thing to

model. BE YOURSELF! YOU ARE AMAZING – LET ALL THAT AMAZINGNESS FLOW!!!

In preparing you to lead, let's talk about something very important – where your responsibility lies toward others.

You are responsible TO love and honor people *through the grace of God*. What that looks like will vary for your children, your spouse, your friend, a leader, a ministry recipient…

But *hear me* on this… there is responsibility you are not to take. Following this will help you and protect you from a world of mess and burn-out!

You are NOT responsible FOR anyone except yourself, with the help of Holy Spirit. You are NOT responsible for others':

- actions
- attitudes
- behaviors
- reactions
- decisions
- total well-being…

THAT is a God level responsibility.

When you take that on – it will soon feel VERY heavy because that job is a God level job.

Usually we do this through lack of understanding, but sometimes it is because we have a need to be needed. The need to be needed is the definition of codependency. Let Holy Spirit help YOU with this if this is a pattern. He wants you free! When we take responsibility for others, we undercut their ability to take responsibility for themselves as appropriate, with His help. This is unhealthy on all sides.

Regularly check to see if you feel the weight of someone else on you. If you feel *heavy*, release that person to the very capable hands of God. Whatever part He wants you to play in being responsible to love and honor them, He will equip you for that and can clearly let you know what that looks like practically.

If you have found you have slipped into this at any time, no condemnation. But keep this prayer handy to release them:

Prayer to Release Responsibility for someone:

> *Lord, I ask you to forgive me for trying to do Your job in _____ life. I realize that in being responsible for _____, I became God with all the weight that comes with being God. I release _____ back to You with all the weight of his/her life. You be God. You be responsible for _____. I'll be responsible to _____. I release him/her to You now and I let him/her go with all the weight of his/her life. In Jesus' name, amen.*

It is HUGELY important that you set appropriate boundaries for those you minister to. If this is a new thing for you, take some time to learn and grow in this area.

I routinely recommend two books to address this topic:

Boundaries: When to Say Yes, How to Say No To Take Control of Your Life by Henry Cloud and John Townsend

Keep Your Love On: Connection, Communication, And Boundaries By Danny Silk

These are masterful works and a gift for everyone, not just ministry leaders. I consider them required reading.

But with all that said, Holy Spirit is the One to help people connect with Him, heal and deliver people, and provide for people. You were intended to live freely and lightly, depending upon Him. One of my all-time favorite verses, Matthew 11:28-30 (MSG) says:

> *Are you tired? Worn out? Burned out on religion? Come to me. Get away with me and you'll recover your life. I'll show you how to take a real rest. Walk with me and work with me—watch how I do it. Learn the unforced rhythms*

of grace. I won't lay anything heavy or ill-fitting on you. Keep company with me and you'll learn to live freely and lightly.

If you make encountering Love your FIRST priority, you will automatically be able to help others operating from that place! It will be a *joy* to give out of what you have received!!!

Make it your aim to be a student of Love first! This is also YOUR course because it is all about Love and none of us knows the depths of Him – there is always more! So be open to receiving, not just giving. Love is all about you – not about what you do for Him!

Okay, Ready, Set, Go...Practicalities

Marked by Love, The Course is divided up into 10 modules. Each module has:

- a video ranging from just under 30 minutes to just over 70 minutes.
- an mp3 downloadable audio file for those that want to listen "on the run".
- a downloadable workbook chapter for each student to digest with Love Encounter Breaks to engage directly with God.

Additional Resources:

As a Marked by Love Course Leader, you will be provided with the *Marked by Love* book as part of your purchase. The chapters parallel the workbook and course. The book contains material which is not in the downloadable workbook and will help you in your personal growth as well as leading your group. The workbook included in your course goes deeper into activations and encountering God.

You can choose to order a *Marked by Love* workbook on Amazon if you would prefer to use that vs. the downloadable workbook. They are the same in content, so that is strictly up to you. Some students will also prefer the softcover *Marked by Love* workbook as well, and it is helpful to have a copy to show them in case they do.

Make sure you show the students the softcover *Marked by Love* book, in case they want to that as an additional resource, as well as a softcover *Marked by Love* workbook if you decide to purchase one for yourself.

For any of the softcover resources, you can either direct students to Amazon to purchase on their own or order for the whole group and collect monies to cover their purchases.

The Group Pace & First Meeting Considerations:

You can choose to take your group through the course as quickly or as slowly as you feel led. However, I would not go faster than one module a week, so that the content can be digested, and the students can take a decent amount of time to go through the workbook and encounter God personally.

I suggest that you begin your first meeting with getting to know the members of your group and what expectations you have for the course. I would play the Welcome video and pass out any materials you want to start with.

What You Will Need:

- a computer/laptop
- a decent internet connection
- ideally a larger screen (TV, overhead…) to connect to
- a reasonably private room with seating
- access to a printer and printer supplies if you will be downloading workbook modules
- If you will be having babysitting, a place for the kids and their babysitter(s)
- Refreshments are optional – simple is usually best

Considerations Before You Start:

- If you will download the modules for the students each week, or have them purchase their own workbook (available on Amazon or www.catherinetoon.com).

- You should also decide if you will have them purchase a *Marked by Love* book as well (available on Amazon or www.catherinetoon.com).
- The frequency you would like to meet (weekly, bi-weekly, etc.). **Please Note:** There will be 11 meetings total.
- where you will meet (at one location or move around).
- If you will have a co-leader to help out, or alternate facilitating the meetings.
- If you will provide refreshments. My advice is to keep it really simple, so you don't get bogged down. If someone has a gift in this area, by all means, take advantage of that.
- If you/your organization will provide any babysitting or allow little ones to be present.
- Whether or not you will take a fee to cover the costs of refreshments, downloadable materials, any babysitting, or any workbooks/books.
- How long you want to meet – 2 hours or less should be more than adequate, unless you want some extended prayer time or socializing.

Login/Password Permissions:

Do not share your login/password with group. This is yours to share with your spouse, if you are married. If you represent a church/organization who purchased the course, that information can be passed along to ***other leaders*** facilitating the course.

Thank you for honoring me and my team in this!

Proposed Overall Meeting Schedule & Structure

Remember this is YOUR course, so make this work for you and your group. However, the expectation is that each student will go through the workbook module readings and Love Encounter Breaks during the week, after watching each video module as a group. I would plan for 2 hours for each meeting, with flexibility.

This course works well if you have a minimum of 1 week in between meetings. If you are reading the chapters in the *Marked by Love* book (optional), along with doing the *Marked by Love* workbook readings and the Love Encounter Breaks, you may want to consider 2 weeks in between, especially if people are falling behind and need more time.

You really want people to give the Love Encounter Breaks some *good quality time*. Transformation happens as *the heart is impacted*. The Love Encounter Breaks are designed to be *luxuriated in,* not checked off a hurried get-through list. However, I don't recommend you spread out the meetings longer than every 2 weeks, as you can lose momentum and people may lose interest.

Whatever the frequency of the meetings, a good meeting schedule would look like:

Sample Meeting

>Prayer +/- worship
>Passing out printed module lessons
>Sign up for new members in class & also for those who want to sign up to join the *Marked by Love* global closed community on Facebook
>Sharing and discussion about previous week's module
>Watch video for this week's module
>Prayer
>Socializing

>Individual Application Time at home: Current week's module of the workbook (and book if desired)

Community Forum

There is a closed community page strictly for Marked by Love Students on Facebook, which is a forum where individuals can share their journey in a safe, supportive environment. Students and Leaders can celebrate one another

and help each other over stumbling blocks. I will be ministering on this page directly as well.

Guidelines for Using This Forum:

The purpose of this page is for the Marked by Love community to be able to share experiences, encourage each other, and develop friendships. Please feel free to totally be yourself!

- Any comments meant to harass, threaten or abuse an individual.
- Content determined to be spam, business solicitation, inappropriate, in poor taste, or otherwise contrary to the purposes of the forum.

We want this to be a safe, life-giving, fun place for our Marked by Love family. Thank you for honoring the heart of this forum! Know that you are LOVED - not only by God, but by us!

Each leader will be emailed instructions with how to join. Each member of your group is encouraged to join the community as well. For those who are interested, please email us a list of their names and email addresses. You can send this list to: admin@catherinetoon.com. We will email your students directly with instructions on how they can join.

As a Leader, YOU need support as well. If there is anything we can help you with, email us at: admin@catherinetoon.com

General Preparation for Each Class:

Make sure that you go through the workbook and video content *before* each class. Even though you are receiving as you go, you should be at least one step ahead of the class, so you can minister out of what you have been getting. In other words, you should be ahead of the class and prepared to lead, even though you will probably still be processing through much of what you are getting. With that, don't feel that you have to have this down, but the video/workbook content should not come as a surprise to you in class.

If you feel you need more time to go through everything, consider having class every 2 weeks, or having a weekly class, but staying on the same module for 2 weeks so that everyone has time to work through it. Use your best judgment.

Also, you should review the Leaders' Guide as well for each module ahead of time, to prepare for each class. Know your personality. Some people are planners and like to have everything prepared way ahead of time. Others tend to be last minute and that is when their creative juices and energy really start to flow. But with that, you should know what you need to be well prepared and give it more time than you initially think. This should be FUN, not a last-minute stress!

What is Your Role?

As a leader for the *Marked by Love* course, your role is not to teach, as much as to facilitate discussion and interaction, as well as organize and coordinate. If your group is larger than around 10 – 12 participants, the group should split up into smaller groups with a leader assigned to each subgroup. Not many will feel comfortable sharing in a group larger than 10 – 12 and everyone is important and should be heard.

Each leader's job is to ensure the safety of the group so that people are free to share experiences, encourage each other, develop friendships, and most of all, be encouraged and freed up to totally be their authentic selves. Strict and authentic confidentiality (no gossiping under the guise of a prayer list) should be maintained. The exception to this, is if someone is a danger to themselves or someone else, your church Pastor or the authorities need to be informed.

Your *Marked by Love* course environment should be one where people celebrate one another and honor each other's viewpoints, personalities, and where each person is in their development. People should be free to disagree, but love and respect should be paramount, even with passionate disagreement.

Aside from all the sober guidelines, have FUN with this. Laughter is freeing and an expression of Love!!

Be personally involved, without relinquishing leadership. Your role is that of a fellow disciple, sharing in struggles just as every student. Authentically sharing this is such a relief to many, who may think you have everything together. However, you are still the leader. If someone tries to take over this role, you need to make it clear that you appreciate their giftings and calls, but you are the one called to lead. Allow for Holy Spirit to lead the class with flexibility, but do not allow discussions to veer off target. Keep the focus on the module's content and application.

Try to create a relaxed atmosphere where everyone belongs.

Open each meeting with prayer to focus the group and be sensitive to what Holy Spirit is doing and directing in the meeting. Jesus gets to be Lord! Ask people to share what God is showing/has shown them. Celebrate this and the person sharing. This encourages everyone and makes it a safe place for others to share.

Make sure that no one, including you, are dominating the discussion. Redirect the discussion when this occurs.

Be an encourager and accept *everyone* right where they are! No one needs to clean up to be loved and accepted. If there are safety issues – emotional/physical/spiritual – you will need to step up to the plate to correct those. But outside of that, Holy Spirit is the Sanctifier and He really does not need us to take that on ourselves!

Love is an inclusive God!

Acknowledge that it takes courage to share. Something like, "Wow! That took a lot of courage and I admire you for sharing!" – goes a long way.

If people need additional ministry, offer some group prayer and follow up as needed. Don't hesitate to meet with them to help them find additional resources. You should not feel pressured to meet all the needs represented in your group. For specific help refer to the **TIPS FOR MINISTERING TO**

NEEDIER INDIVIDUALS & **ADDITIONAL RESOURCES** sections at the end of the guide.

With this, boundaries are super important. No one should be forced to share or do anything else forcibly, only encouraged. Remember too, that you are not the Source. Make sure you know what you can give in terms of prayer support, etc. Say what you can and are willing to do and set limits. Encourage students to pray with one another, but also to set boundaries as well.

End your group sharing and discussion periods on time. You will need to give this expectation during your first meeting. People can stay and mingle more if that works for the people who are hosting. If not, encourage the students to mingle outside the meeting. Practical ways to end a meeting on time:

- Keep track of the time. If this is hard for you, assign someone to remind you 5 minutes before the closing time.
- If someone is talking, interrupt them saying – "This is so good, but I need to let you know we only have 5 more minutes left. Thanks so much for sharing." If there is a lot left, you can ask them to bring it up the next meeting.

Remind people that the discussions are confidential, but to encourage students to pray for one another during the intervals between modules.

There are People, There are Problems (But People are not Problems) - Coping Strategies:

Keep in mind, that no matter how well run and anointed your group is, and with as much energy you pour in, there will still be issues that come up. Take it to the Lord, He is well able to give an edifying correction, if needed, but most likely it is NOT personal! If you find you are taking on responsibility FOR (vs. TO love and honor) the members of your group – release them to the Lord with the *Prayer to Release Responsibility*. They are His beloved sheep!

Absenteeism – Call them, or have the subgroup leader call them, to express concern and encourage them to make up the exercises so that they will not fall too behind and get discouraged and drop out.

Not Completing the Workbook Assignments at Home – Emphasize at your Introductory Meeting that the majority of the impact comes from each student going through the workbook and engaging with God through the exercises. If someone has not completed the workbook assignments, encourage them to keep up to date with the current exercises and catch up.

If someone is attending and not doing the workbook, but they are receiving and contributing in class, encourage them to dive in. Call them or have your sub-group leader call them and discuss what the issues are. Help where you can. If they are still not doing the work but are receiving plenty in the class as-is, *and* they are not a hindrance to the rest of the class, it should not be a problem for them to continue.

However, if it looks like someone repeatedly is not doing the work, you have done all of the above, and their lack of preparation is dragging down the group, you may want to lovingly suggest that they withdraw and participate at a time when they are less overwhelmed and can devote themselves more.

Here are some tips for completing the workbook (This is part of my personal note to the students, but please be sure to go over this with your class during your first meeting):

- Stay current with each week, at least partially
- Finishing each week is a priority, if you are getting more in a particular exercise, come back to it later so you can finish the week and won't get bogged down
- Skip over exercises that you are struggling with and come back to them later
- Remember that everyone can come back and redo the exercises as situations change – the Lord ALWAYS has more to say! This is not a one-shot deal!

- Be honest with yourself about how much time the workbook will take. This is more about luxuriating in the truths Love is giving you, not checking off your exercise list. This is worth adequate time!
- Don't wait until the night before the next meeting to start. This will keep you from stressing. If you are more of a last-minute person, you may want to make your deadline 2 nights before the session (kind of like setting your clock 15 minutes before you want to get up, knowing you will hit the snooze button). This will help you - you can do this!

Disagreements – they are healthy and will happen. Your *Marked by Love* course environment should be one where people celebrate one another and honor each other's viewpoints, personalities, and where each person is in their development. People should be free to disagree, but love and respect should be paramount, even with passionate disagreement. Scripture, rightly interpreted, gets to be the final authority. If the debate becomes counterproductive, suggest that the parties (including you, if an issue), continue the discussion later, so that the class is kept on track.

If someone is expecting you to be an authority and answer all questions, emphasize that you are facilitating discussion and not the be-all authority. If the issue seems weighty, you can ask someone to research it, or take that task on if you feel led.

Group Domination – make sure this is not you. Group domination may look like:

- Claiming an inordinate amount of the meeting time to talk about their issues
- Repeatedly waiting until the last 10 minutes to introduce an emotionally-charged issue
- Challenging your leadership in a hostile way
- Criticizing others' motives or feelings

Your job is to facilitate opportunities for everyone to share. If someone is dominating the time:

- Ask someone to share who has not shared yet
- Focus directly on someone else
- Directly say, "Thank you ____, let's give everyone the opportunity to share. ____ what have you found?"

If someone is going into too much detail and losing the interest of the class, discreetly interrupt the person: "So what you are trying to say is _____. "You can also restate the question, "So ____, What did God show you about …?"

If someone repeatedly is challenging your authority, you can say, "I understand you disagree, let's discuss this after the meeting, or at a later date." At that time, one - on - one, you can simply, non-defensively, let them know that you are the one that God chose/was chosen to lead the class, and that you trust that your authority will be respected even if they disagree. Ask if there is something specific that is making them uncomfortable. Give them a chance to express themselves. This will often diffuse the situation. If they, or you, are still not comfortable with the situation, tell them it is probably best that they join a group that they feel more comfortable with.

Keep in mind, you may get some good feedback either way, to take to the Lord as a part of your learning curve. But do not take everything personally. Wounded people can come with all sorts of agendas that are not God's agenda. At the end of the day, you were the one God picked to lead, end of that particular discussion.

Woundedness, Trauma and Crises – people come with all sorts of backgrounds, trauma, woundedness, and crises. Survivors of trauma do need to talk about their pain, but lengthy emotional processing is not the point of the course meetings. Because it is so important that people feel loved, validated, and not shut down, I prepared a letter, personally from me to help with this. You will find it on pg. 141 at the back of the Leaders' Guide. It should be run off and passed out to each member when they join at the first meeting.

As a leader, the idea that you can help someone can be very seductive, and you may feel great pressure to direct the group to spend inordinate time to help a particularly hurting member.

Remember you/the group are not responsible FOR the person. You are responsible TO love and honor the person, but you/the group are not the Source!

After an initial small amount of time, redirect the group back to the course and let the person know you will talk to them individually. The course is not designed to be counseling or a specific support group. Plan to meet with the person to help them get the assistance they need. Remember, this is about encountering Love directly – not being Holy Spirit, Jr. or a specific support group. Please refer to my Additional Tips for Needier Individuals and Resources at the back of this guide.

Demonic Manifestations - Yeah, they happen sometimes. Do not allow the enemy to show off on Love's time. Big God, little devil. Perfect Love casts out fear (1 John 4:18). Stay calm, take a deep breath, and quiet the group. Thank God for being so huge and taking care of _____. Command the demon(s) to be silent, if they happen to be mouthing off (big mouths, little devils). Continue to thank God for His hugeness and goodness and power. FOCUS ON *LOVE*! Thank Him that His perfect love casts out fear and command the spirit of fear to go, in Jesus's name. There is no need to yell – none of the parties are deaf, and loud does not mean anointed. Say firmly, "In the name of Jesus, I command this unholy presence to leave ____ and this group right now. You are not allowed here. Thank You, Jesus that you gave us power to trample on serpents and scorpions and over *all* the power of the enemy and that nothing shall by any means harm us (Luke 10:19). You are so good and have nothing but good for your son/daughter. Thank You that you are Love and Love always wins (1 Corinthians 13:8)!!!! Thank You that you always back us up! In Jesus's name! Amen."

Hebrews 13:5b (AMPC) says:

> *For He [God] Himself has said, I will not in any way fail you nor give you up nor leave you without support. [I will] not, [I will] not, [I will] not in any degree leave you helpless nor forsake nor let [you] down (relax My hold on you)! [Assuredly not!]*

Praise God with the group to shift the atmosphere and assure everyone who might have been shaken. Assure the individual that you will help them after the meeting. Then resume the meeting.

Make sure you have the individual follow up with some wholeness ministry, so that the underlying reasons the enemy was able to attach to the individual are taken care of. Demons are like rats attracted to garbage. If you cast out a rat from a garbage pile, it may well just come back. If the garbage is taken care of, the "rats" may sniff around, but they have no place to attach themselves. THIS is not your job! But if the demonic manifests on your time, make sure they know that YOU KNOW that Love does not tolerate them on His time!!!

If there is demonic activity that has been sent to upset the meeting, use your authority to speak against whatever you are discerning (witchcraft, confusion, strife…). The sons of God are led by the Spirit of God. If you need backup, call your church security or 911 to escort the individual(s) out. This is not typical, but it can happen with anointed meetings. At the beginning, middle and end of the day, Jesus is Lord - big God, little devil. You have not been given a spirit of fear, but of HUGE power, ENDLESS love and a sound mind OF CHRIST. YOU have been given His authority!

The enemy is terrified of a believer who knows who they are and whose they are! Be at peace! All is not only well, but sooooo amazing! LOVE is IN YOU (Colossians 1:27), You are ONE WITH LOVE (1 Corinthians 6:17), and you are utterly IN LOVE (Colossians 3:3-4, Galatians 3:26-27)!! YOU can't lose for winning (Romans 8:37).

Coordinating a Larger Group:

If you are coordinating a larger group with multiple smaller subgroups, you will need to do more planning and involve leadership in any organizations/churches that you are doing this through. You will want to have earlier sign ups and determine facilitators for sub-groups. And you will want to meet with those leaders to plan, get curriculum, figure out space, and share the vision and guidelines, so that you operate as one team. You may well need to track attendance if required and procure audio/visual support.

I recommend you make the process as simple and as informal as possible. This is not a conference or a formal teaching venue. It is a chance for people to encounter Love in more intimate ways than they ever thought possible.

MODULE 1

Introduction

God is love. By this the love of God was in us, that God has sent His only begotten Son into the world so that we might live through Him.
1 John 4:8-9 (NASB)

Ministry for You as a Leader – First Things First

Whohoo - you are on your way, not only as a leader, but as a recipient first! This is YOUR course because it is all about Love. And Love is all about you!

As you prepare to lead your first module, this is a good time to gauge where YOU as a leader are and what you want to get out of YOUR course, as well as what you want to see happen for your students.

Love wants to be known and He wants *you* to know Him *first* and release to your students from t*hat* place. You will be growing together with your students and authenticity here will be precious and give hope to your students. It will also point to Him as the Source, not you – whew! *Pressure off!*

As much as God wants to be known, this is not a reality many people experience, or experience often. They get stuck. If this is you, no problem, even as a leader. Get ready for an upgrade!

Now is a good time to check to see how easy it is for *you* to connect to God. Where do you get stuck when you try to hear from or connect with God?

There are multiple areas where people tend to break down when trying to connect with God. I have compiled a list for you to do a heart check with. It is a truth that we live out of what we believe in our hearts, not what we know in our heads. This is what Jesus meant when He said in John 8:32:

Then you will know the truth. And the truth will set you free.

Here are truths and non-exhaustive scriptural references that you can study out for yourself, to prepare yourself to lead the first introductory class:

- God readily speaks/connects to people today (Jeremiah 29:11-13; Jeremiah 33:3; John 16:13).
- Hearing from/connecting to God regularly is the birthright for ALL believers (2 Corinthians 1:1 AMP; Jeremiah 29:11-13; Jeremiah 33:3; John 16:13). Note: By scriptural definition, all believers are called saints.
- Hearing from/connecting with God is not a sovereign thing – except that God sovereignly chose to reconcile back to His kids. Like any conversation between parents and their children, we can initiate the conversation (Jeremiah 29:11-13; Jeremiah 33:3; Matthew 7:7-8).
- God does not require you to fast, worship, confess sins… in order to hear from Him, but you are welcome to if you want or if it helps you (Psalms 91:15; 2 Corinthians 5:17-19; Galatians 5:1).
- Yes, God is holy, but sin separates *us* from *Him*, NOT *Him* from *us*. And that separation is *only in our minds*. He will speak/connect with you right in the midst of sin – you may need it the most then! He calls the believer righteous and helps them walk in freedom from sin (Colossians 1:20-22; Psalms 91:15; 2 Corinthians 5:17-22; Hebrews 9:14; Hebrews 10:22; 1 Corinthians 15:34).
- God is not angry and wrathful. Jesus in the flesh was the express image of His Father - Father God (Hebrews 1:1-3).
- Connecting/talking to you was His idea! You are the joy set before Him! (Genesis 3:8; Hebrews 12:2; Jeremiah 29:11-13; Jeremiah 33:3; John 16:13).
- God is always there to talk and commune with you (Jeremiah 33:3; Matthew 7:7-11; John 10:3,16,27).
- God speaks to everyone including "sinners" (Matthew 18:12; Colossians 1:20-22; 1 John 2:2; John 12:47).
- If it sounds like you, it may well be Holy Spirit speaking through your spirit – your spirit sounds like you (Colossians 1:27, 1 John 2:20; 1 Corinthians 6:17).
- If it is really, really good – too good to be true, it sounds just like God and His gospel (Ephesians 2:7; Ephesians 3:20).
- You can talk to God about the big things and the smallest small details. If it matters to you, it matters to Him! (Matthew 10:29-31, Psalms 139:17-18).

- You can totally distinguish between God, yourself, and the devil (John 10:27, 1 John 2:20, Hebrews 5:14) – you may just need help!
- The devil cannot separate the believer from God. He can't even separate the unbeliever from God if they don't want to be (Romans 8:38-39; John 17:11; John 18:9; Mark 5:1-6; 1 Corinthians 6:17; Ephesians 2:6).
- There is no particular position to hear from/connect with God. Get comfortable so you won't be distracted – just maybe not lying down if you are sleepy (Psalm 4:4; Psalm 63:6; Psalms 91:15; Psalms 139:7-13; Isaiah 50:4).
- If it is God, it should sound like Love, peace, and joy – God is scriptural, but not staid, stale or religious. If we "hear" Him that way and it has no life, it is probably because we struggle with religious overlay, or we may struggle connecting to our own hearts. Love will meet us where we are. He can totally help us get past all that (Zephaniah 3:17; Isaiah 9:6; 1 Corinthians 13:4-8)!
- God is sometimes serious, but His Kingdom is joy and He loves to laugh – just like us! He is also very relaxed – He can afford to be (Zephaniah 3:17; Isaiah 9:6; 1 Corinthians 13:4-8; Romans 14:17; Hebrews 1:3; Hebrews 10:12)!
- You were born to hear from/connect with God (Jeremiah 29:11-13; Jeremiah 33:3; John 10:3, 16-17; John 16:13; Psalms 91:15).
- You were born to hear from/connect with God *well* and should expect to do so regularly (Jeremiah 29:11-13; Jeremiah 33:3; John 10:3, 16-17; John 16:13; Psalms 91:15; Ephesians 2:6).
- Hearing from/connecting with God should look/feel like righteousness, peace and joy, but most of all it should feel like love (1 Kings 19:12; Zephaniah 3:17; Isaiah 9:6; Romans 14:17; 1 Corinthians 13:4-8; Colossians 3:15).
- The ability to hear from/connect with God is something you are born with and it is something that should be trained and developed (Hebrews 5:14; Ephesians 1:18). Practice and more practice will make you a pro.
- Hearing from/connecting with God may or may not feel supernatural. It's natural to connect with your Father, Friend, Husband and Comforter, but you are also a supernatural being – a spirit seated in heavenly places

in Christ (1 Kings 19:12; Zephaniah 3:17; Isaiah 9:6; 1 Corinthians 13:4-8; Colossians 3:15; Ephesians 2:6).
- If you've asked over and over, but haven't heard/connected to God, it isn't that He isn't speaking or showing you things. There's a breakdown, but it is not on God's end. He is faithful!

  - You may have bad doctrine that you didn't know to question. This will hinder you unless you reject it and renew your mind to what the scripture is saying in the context of the whole of scripture, the history/culture surrounding it, and the actual audience it was written to. You will need to allow yourself to be challenged and study it out for yourself.
  - You may be having a hard time discerning when God is speaking to you/connecting with you. This is particularly an issue with people who connect with God through their thoughts, but it may be an issue with any of the ways that people connect as primary or secondary modalities:

    - spiritual sight
    - spiritual hearing
    - spiritual touch
    - spiritual taste/smell
    - internal knowing
    - thoughts
    - peace
    - angelic encounters
    - supernatural signs/wonders
    - dreams

  This is just a training and practice issue.

  - You may be offended with God and blocking it consciously or subconsciously.
  - You may be fearful of God and blocking it consciously or subconsciously.

- You may be struggling with a sense of unworthiness and shame and blocking it consciously or subconsciously.

Whatever the deal is, God will help you get past it! Be encouraged! Unless you are on a mission to prove that God really is not upholding His end of the bargain and aren't willing to get past it, you are a prime candidate for Love's unfair trump card – His grace! He will help you if you will just stick with it (Numbers 23:19; Jeremiah 29:11-13; Jeremiah 33:3; John 10:3, 16-17; John 14:6; John 16:13; 2 Timothy 2:13)! I've seen it over and over. I am excited for you and want to hear about your victories as they happen!!

If none of these seem to describe where you are – awesome! But there is always more, and you should not be content just to stay where you are.

Father, I thank You for shoring up any areas where each leader is hindered in connecting to You personally for themselves. You desire robust, unfettered relationship with Your son/daughter first and foremost, before their service. Thank You for making this such a dynamic, life-giving experience for them personally! I take authority over any agendas that are not Your agenda for the meetings and for them personally! You are well able to protect and bless and move for them and through them mightily in ways they have never experienced before! I thank You for blessing their heart to serve and I thank you for pouring out wisdom in every situation and meeting! Thank You that Your Presence lingers on them and goes before them for each meeting! Thank You for providing all the help and resources they need! Thank You for the breakthroughs and encounters You will minister to them and through them! Thank You for causing them to encounter You in ways they never thought possible! In Jesus's wondrous name! Amen!!!

Goals of Meeting – 1st Session

Administrative Goals:

- Register students

- When new people come throughout the course, remember to get all their contact information & make sure you give them the *Personal Note from Catherine*
- Distribute any materials
- Take any orders (workbooks/books) & collect monies if needed (workbooks/book/ babysitting/refreshment fees)
  After class: promptly order workbooks/books
- Discuss the optional *Marked by Love* closed Facebook forum & note students' preferences
  After class: turn in information to admin@catherinetoon.com for those interested in joining the community

Ministry Goals:

- WELCOME EVERYONE
- Prayer/+ or - worship
- Get to know one another - have new members introduce themselves – Ice Breaker/Remove the Mask exercise
- Explain the basics, review expectations, and review the format of the meetings
- View Video: **Module 1: Introduction** (27 min.)
- General Discussion
- Close in prayer/socializing if desired

Before the Meeting – 1ˢᵗ Session

- Carefully review all of the **Welcome Leaders Section**
- Complete *Marked by Love* **Workbook Module 1**
- I strongly suggest that you review *Marked by Love* book – Introduction. This will help your confidence in leading your class and be a huge blessing to you.
- Carefully review the **During the Session: 1ˢᵗ Meeting** so you are prepared.

- Pray for wisdom, guidance and inspiration as you lead; be open to any words from the Lord to share with the class. He always has something delightful to say.
- You will have access to an optional *Marked by Love* Closed Community forum on Facebook just for *Marked by Love* students/leaders. Here, you'll be able to share and have fun connecting with your new global *Marked by Love* family. You will also be able to support one another, if issues arise. Catherine will also be ministering live and sharing other content intermittently via this venue. I recommend you check this out for yourself early. Your students can individually choose to join as well. This is offered for free by Imprint (the ministry the Marked by Love series comes from). Pass out the registration sheet to have people sign up for this.

    - FOR YOU ONLY: As a leader, you can request to join, and we will approve you.
    - FOR YOUR STUDENTS: When you provide the names and emails of any students desiring to participate, we will send them information directly and will approve their request, when they submit it to us.

- Make sure the room is set up appropriately, the audio-visual equipment is working (laptop; connection to a screen; mic if using, etc.)
- Run off copies of the download for **Module 1: Introduction** (make sure you have plenty of copies)
- Run off plenty of copies of *Personal Note from Catherine*

During the Meeting – 1st Session

- Prayer/+ or - worship
- WELCOME everyone and introduce yourself and any leaders or administrators
- Register students:

This can be anything from passing a sheet around to a formal registration process at your organization.
I recommend getting at least:

- full names
- phone numbers
- emails
- permission to share those within the group, if desired (not everyone has to share), so that people can support one another and pray outside the meeting

- Because students often will want to contact other students for prayer and support, let them know that group contact information can be shared by those who give their individual permission.
- As you do this, get to know people – go around and introduce yourself. Ask people to share who they are, what they want from the class.
- Do an ICE BREAKER to get people comfortable and to get to know one another. The goal is to laugh! Ha Ha Ha - If it's not fun, just say "no"! Choose from the list in the back of this guide or make up your own.
- Get your registration sheet back and make sure all have filled it out; let them know you will pass out contact information to the group for those that gave permission next time.
- Explain the basics, review expectations, and review the format of the meetings – keep it short and sweet – minimize the boring.
- Distribute any materials:

  - Downloadable workbook pdf for **Module 1**. If for some reason you run out, email people a copy.
  - Make *sure* you give them the *Personal Note from Catherine* – if for some reason you run out, email people a copy.

- Tell them that they will be watching the video for **Module 1** today.
- Stress that the expectation and real impact of the course will happen as they go through the workbook for **Module 1** *before* the next meeting *on their own*.

- Emphasize this is not homework as much as it is a time to receive ministry directly from the Lord. Urge them to plan now when they will start it and put it on their calendar. Give them a few minutes to look at their schedule and think about this.
- Have them read through the *Personal Note from Catherine*. Reiterate with great compassion that we all have crises and we all need extra help at times. It is a brave, beautiful, and godly thing to seek professional help when we need it. They are totally worth it. Explain that this course is designed to be loving, supportive, and safe. However, this is not a support group, nor does it replace counseling or other forms of help. During the week we encourage people to pray for one another, but this also does not replace professional help, and appropriate boundaries need to be maintained. Tell everyone to come see you if there are issues they need help with and you will do your best to help or connect them with help. (5 – 10 min. to read and discuss)
- Also, go over tips for completing the workbook.
- Tell the group, that the *Marked by Love* environment needs to be safe for people to authentically share. That means **total confidentiality** unless there is harm to self or others at stake. What is said in class stays in class. No gossiping in the name of prayer chains!
- The name of the game is authentic sharing, keeping it real. Safe, life-giving, and fun! Even if there are painful things that come up, laughter will help everyone through.
- Have everyone stand up. Say, "We are going to play the **Remove the Mask Game.**" Tell them "We are going to remove the "Church-Face" / "I'm-happy-when-I'm-not-Face" because we want to see, celebrate and help the real you. So, on the count of 3, we are going rip off the 'Church-Face'/'I'm-happy-when-I'm-not-Face' and throw them in a pile at the front of the room and I'm going to torch them with a make-believe lighter. NOW – for those of you, *for whom this is not safe yet*, feel free to imagine a mask behind the mask to keep you safe. The rest of you – just rip it off and laugh!"

Demonstrate.

Then count, 1 – 2 – 3 throw it in the heap and torch it!
Most everyone will be laughing. Watch for those for whom this is hard and keep a mental note to protect and give them special help.

Tell them *we will do this every week* so that they will become master mask-ripper-offers and start to learn to live as their authentic selves.

Say "For those of you, who this was hard, or you needed a mask behind the mask, this will be a huge step for you to live as your authentic self. This will come with time as you feel more and more safe."

Tell them that God wants us whole, free, safe, and connected with who we really are. He wants you to be comfortable in your own skin because you are settled that you are lovely, powerful, and secure in who you are. He will be helping you masterfully with just that. Tell them that you will be standing with them in this process!

- Discuss whether you will be using the softcover *Marked by Love* workbook or recommending the *Marked by Love* book.
- Take any orders with monies for:

    - softcover *Marked by Love* workbooks (if desired)
    - *Marked by Love* books (if desired)

    Note: You can also have everyone order their own copies of either the softcover *Marked by Love* workbook or the *Marked by Love* book directly from Amazon, or on my website https://catherinetoon.com.

- Discuss that they can have access to an optional *Marked by Love* Closed Community forum on Facebook just for *Marked by Love* students/leaders. Here, they'll be able to share and have fun connecting with their new global *Marked by Love* family. They will also be able to support one another, if issues arise. Catherine will also be ministering live and sharing other content intermittently via this venue.

- Pass around the registration form so people can circle their names if they are interested in checking it out.
- After class, you should email us at: **admin@catherinetoon.com** providing us with the names and emails of any students desiring to participate. We will promptly send them all the information they need and will approve their request, when they submit it to us.

- VIEW FIRST MODULE VIDEO: *Introduction – "Setting Yourself up for Love Encounters"* (approximately 27 min.)
- Give a 5-min. stretch/bathroom break

General Discussion – facilitated by you, encouraging all students to share and no one to dominate the conversation:

- Help students start to become aware that we all have faulty understanding and perceptions of God and how He relates to us personally. This creates filters that compromise our connection with Him. Awareness is the first step in overcoming these.
- Ask them if they have experienced this.
- Help students start to become aware of stumbling blocks that come from personal experience or lack thereof. These are impeding our connection to God experientially.
- Ask what they have run into.
- Help your students to explore what spiritual senses/modalities God primarily connects to them through:
    - Spiritual sight
    - Spiritual hearing
    - Spiritual touch
    - Spiritual taste
    - Spiritual smell
    - Internal knowing/Inner Witness
    - Thoughts/Mind of Christ
    - Peace

- - Angelic/Supernatural signs/Supernatural wonders

- Ask them how they think God primarily connects to them. If they are not sure, reassure them they will be getting a lot of help and practice throughout the course. Practice… practice… practice.

  - Consider sharing a little of your experience with hearing God.

- Encourage them to practice their primary modality and lean on God to expand to other modalities:
- Share tips for completing the workbook:

  - Stay current with each week at least partially; since you are part of a class, you want to be able to keep up with the class at least partially.
  - Finishing each week is a priority, if you are getting more in a particular exercise, come back to it later so you can finish the week and won't get bogged down.
  - Skip over exercises that you are struggling with and come back to them later.
  - Remember that everyone can come back and redo the exercises as situations change – the Lord ALWAYS has more to say! This is not a one-shot deal!
  - Be honest with yourself about how much time the workbook will take. This is more about luxuriating in the truths Love is giving you and your students, not checking off your exercise list. This is worth adequate time!
  - Don't wait until the night before the next meeting to start. This will keep you from stressing. If you are more of a last-minute person, make your deadline 2 nights before the meeting. This will help you – you can do this!

- Allow people to ask questions and give short prayer requests.
- Close in prayer/give time for socializing if desired.

CONGRATULATIONS YOU AND YOUR GROUP ARE ON YOUR WAY!!

After the Meeting – 1st Session

- Gather your sign-up sheets
- Answer questions

MODULE 2

The Epicenter of Universe

God is love. By this the love of God was in us, that God has sent His only begotten Son into the world so that we might live through Him.
1 John 4:8-9 (NASB)

Goals of the Meeting – 2nd Session

Administrative Goals:

- Register new students
- When new people come throughout the course, remember to get all their contact information & make sure you give them the *Personal Note from Catherine*
- Distribute any materials
- Take any new orders (workbooks/books) & collect monies if needed (workbooks/book/ babysitting/refreshment fees)
  After class: promptly order workbooks/books and fulfill orders
- Discuss the optional *Marked by Love* closed Facebook forum & note students' preferences
  After class: turn in information to <u>admin@catherinetoon.com</u> for those interested in joining the community

Ministry Goals:

- WELCOME EVERYONE
- Prayer/+ or - worship
- Get to know one another more – Ice Breaker/Remove the mask exercise
- General Discussion: **Module 1: Introduction**
- View Video: **Module 2: The Epicenter of the Universe** (34 min.)
- Close in prayer/socializing if desired

Before the Meeting – 2nd Session

- Watch video and complete all of **Module 2 – The Epicenter of the Universe** in *Marked by Love* Workbook.
- Review *Marked by Love* Book **Chapter 1 – The Epicenter of the Universe** (strongly suggested).
- Enjoy receiving and interacting on the closed *Marked by Love* community forum – this is YOUR course too!
- Pray for wisdom, guidance and inspiration as you lead; be open to any words from the Lord to share with the class. He always has something delightful to say.
- Pray for each student by name – speak over them and the class as God leads you. As long as it is blessing and life, trust that He is speaking through you!
- Carefully review the **During the Session: 2nd Meeting** section so you are prepared.
- Make sure any books/workbooks are ordered and bring them to class. If an administrator is doing this, check to make sure this is completed.
- Make sure that names and emails of any students desiring to join the closed *Marked by Love* community forum are emailed to admin@catherinetoon.com.
- Make sure that refreshments have been taken care of.
- Follow up with any students that are needing particular help.
- Prepare a list of contact information to be shared with the group (for people that agreed to share their information) – run off copies for the group, with extra for new students.
- Run off copies of the download for **Module 2: The Epicenter of the Universe** (make sure you have extra for new students).
- Bring extra copies of **Module 1: Introduction** for new students.
- Run off/bring extra copies of *Personal Note from Catherine* for new people.

During the Meeting – 2nd Session

- Prayer/+ or - worship
- WELCOME everyone and introduce yourself and any leaders or administrators to any new students.
- Register new students – let them know that group information can be shared if permission is given:
  This can be anything from passing a sheet around to a formal registration process at your organization.
  I recommend getting at least:

  - full names
  - phone numbers
  - emails
  - permission to share those within the group, if desired (not everyone has to share), so that people can support one another and pray outside the meeting

- As you do this, get to know any new people. Ask new people to briefly share who they are, what they want from the class. Welcome them warmly.
- Do an ICE BREAKER to get people comfortable and to get to know one another. The goal is to laugh! Ha Ha Ha - If it's not fun, just say "no"! Choose from the list in the back of this guide or make up your own.
- Get your new student registration sheet back and make sure all new students have filled it out.
- Distribute any materials:

  - Downloadable workbook pdf for **Module 2 – The Epicenter of the Universe** – if for some reason you run out, email people a copy.
  - Pass out extra copies of workbook pdf **Module 1: Introduction** for new students.
  - Make *sure* you give new people the *Personal Note from Catherine*.
  - Pass out Group Contact Information Sheet.

- Tell them that they will be watching the video for **Module 2** today.
- Remind them of the expectation that they go through the workbook for **Module 2** *before* the next meeting *on their own*. This is where the *real impact* of the course will happen as they encounter Love for themselves!
- Emphasize this is not homework as much as it is a time to receive ministry directly from the Lord.
- Urge them to plan now when they will start it and put it on their calendar. Give them a few minutes to look at their schedule and think about this.
- Tell new people to read through the *Personal Note from Catherine*. Explain that this course is designed to be loving, supportive, and safe. However, this is not a support group, nor does it replace counseling or other forms of help. During the week, we encourage people to pray for one another, but this also does not replace professional help and appropriate boundaries need to be maintained. Remind everyone to come see you if there are issues they need help with and you will do your best to help or connect them with help.
- Remind the group, that the *Marked by Love* environment needs to be safe for people to authentically share. That means **total confidentiality** unless there is harm to self or others at stake. What is said in class stays in class. No gossiping in the name of prayer chains!
- Have everyone stand up. Tell them it is time for the **Remove the Mask Exercise**. Explain to new people that this is a safe place for people to be their authentic selves and that we are going to remove the "Church-Face" / "I'm-happy-when-I'm-not-Face". We want to see, celebrate and help the real you.

"So, on the count of 3, we are going rip off the 'Church-Face'/'I'm-happy-when-I'm-not-Face' and throw them in a pile at the front of the room and I'm going to torch them with a make-believe lighter."

Reiterate, "NOW – for those of you, *for whom this is not safe yet*, feel free to imagine a mask behind the mask to keep you safe. The rest of you can just rip it off and laugh!"

Then count, 1 – 2 – 3 and say, "Rip off your mask and throw it in the heap. Let's torch them!"

Most everyone will be laughing. Watch for those for whom this is hard and keep a mental note to protect and give them special help.

Remind them that *we will do this every week* so that they will become master mask-ripper-offers and start to learn to live as their authentic selves.

Remind everyone, "For those of you this was hard for, or you needed a mask behind the mask, this will be a huge step for you to live as your authentic self. This will come with time as you feel more and more safe."

Tell them that God wants us whole, free, safe, and connected with who we really are. He wants you to be comfortable in your own skin because you are settled that you are lovely, powerful, and secure in who you are. He will be helping you masterfully with just that. Tell them that you will be standing with them in this process!

- Take any orders with monies for new:

    o softcover *Marked by Love* workbooks (if desired)
    o *Marked by Love* books (if desired)

    Note: You can also have anyone order their own copies of either the softcover *Marked by Love* workbook or the *Marked by Love* book directly from Amazon, or on my website https://catherinetoon.com.

- Remind them that they can have access to an optional *Marked by Love* Closed Community forum on Facebook just for *Marked by Love* students/leaders. Here, they'll be able to share and have fun connecting with their new global *Marked by Love* family. They will also be able to support one another, if issues arise. Catherine will be ministering live and sharing other content intermittently via this venue.

- Pass around the registration form again so that people can circle their names if they are interested in checking it out.
- After class you should email us at: **admin@catherinetoon.com** providing us with the names and emails of any new students desiring to participate. We will promptly send them all the information they need and will approve their request, when they submit it to us.

General Discussion – facilitated by you, encouraging all students to share and no one to dominate the conversation:

- Talk about how Love wants to be known by the object of His love!
- Tell them you are going to read from part of the list of truths about God. Ask people to raise their hands if they have struggled to believe the following truths. As people start to raise their hands, ask them why they think that is and let them start sharing. Go through at least 3 truths, but don't try to go through them all. The important thing is to get as many people sharing as you can – not to "get through the material":
    - God readily speaks/connects to people today
    - Hearing from/connecting to God regularly is the birthright for ALL believers, by scriptural definition all believers are called saints.
    - We can initiate conversation with God – no fasting, worshiping, confessing sins… (but you are welcome to if you want).
    - Yes, God is holy, but sin separates *us* from *Him (in our minds)*, NOT *Him* from *us*. He will speak/connect with you right in the midst of sin – you need it most then!
    - You can totally distinguish between God, yourself, or the devil – you may just need help!
    - If it is God, it should sound like Love, peace, and joy – God is scriptural, but not staid, stale or religious. He loves to laugh.

- Ask how many people have asked over and over but have struggled to hear/connect to God. Highlight that breakdowns are not on God's end. He is faithful! Trip-ups come from our end and can be overcome. If you need to go into more, you can elaborate that trip-ups come from:

- bad doctrine that you didn't know to question
- hard time discerning when God is speaking to you/connecting with you
- being offended with God consciously or subconsciously
- being fearful of God consciously or subconsciously.
- struggling with a sense of unworthiness and shame consciously or subconsciously.

• Say that we usually connect with God in a primary way but can connect in multiple ways. Ask how many people connect with God through _____. Ask them to share what that looks like.

- spiritual sight
- spiritual hearing
- spiritual touch
- spiritual taste/smell
- internal knowing
- thoughts
- peace
- angelic encounters
- supernatural signs/wonders
- dreams

• Encourage them to practice, practice, practice with their primary modality and lean on God to expand to other modalities.
• Ask people what God revealed to them about stumbling blocks that interfere with their ease of receiving from/connecting to God as Love.

- Ask what truth He revealed to them about those stumbling blocks.

• Give a 5-min. stretch/bathroom break.
• VIEW VIDEO: **Module 2: "The Epicenter of The Universe":** (approximately 34 min.)

- Discuss that the students will be going over the **Module 2** workbook section before the next meeting.
- As a reminder, and if there are new students, share tips for completing workbook:

  - Stay current with each week at least partially; since you are part of a class, you want to be able to keep up with the class at least partially.
  - Finishing each week is a priority, if you are getting more in a particular exercise, come back to it later so you can finish the week and won't get bogged down.
  - Skip over exercises that you are struggling with and come back to them later.
  - Remember that everyone can come back and redo the exercises as situations change – the Lord ALWAYS has more to say! This is not a one-shot deal!
  - Be honest with yourself about how much time the workbook will take. This is more about luxuriating in the truths Love is giving you and your students, not checking off your exercise list. This is worth adequate time!
  - Don't wait until the night before the next meeting to start. This will keep you from stressing. If you are more of a last-minute person, make your deadline 2 nights before the meeting. This will help you - you can do this!

- Allow people to ask questions and give short prayer requests.
- Close in prayer/give time for socializing if desired.

CONGRATULATIONS YOU COMPLETED THE SECOND MEETING!!

After the Meeting - 2nd Session

- Gather your new sign-up sheets
- Answer questions

MODULE 3

The Flavors of God

God is love. By this the love of God was in us, that God has sent His only begotten Son into the world so that we might live through Him.
1 John 4:8-9 (NASB)

Goals of the Meeting – 3rd Session

Administrative Goals:

- Register new students
- When new people come throughout the course, remember to get all their contact information & make sure you give them the *Personal Note from Catherine*
- Distribute any materials
- Take any new orders (workbooks/books) & collect monies if needed (workbooks/book/ babysitting/refreshment fees)
  After class: promptly order workbooks/books and fulfill orders
- Discuss the optional *Marked by Love* closed Facebook forum & note students' preferences
  After class: turn in information to admin@catherinetoon.com for those interested in joining the community

Ministry Goals:

- WELCOME EVERYONE
- Prayer/+ or – worship
- Get to know one another more – Ice Breaker/Remove the mask exercise
- View Video: **Module 3: The Flavors of God** (39 min.)
- General Discussion
- Close in prayer/socializing if desired

Before the Meeting – 3rd Session

- Watch video and complete all of **Module 3 – The Flavors of God** in *Marked by Love* Workbook.
- Review *Marked by Love* Book **Chapter 2 – The Flavors of God** (strongly suggested).
- Enjoy receiving and interacting on the closed *Marked by Love* community forum – this is YOUR course too!
- Pray for wisdom, guidance and inspiration as you lead; be open to any words from the Lord to share with the class. He always has something delightful to say.
- Pray for each student by name – speak over them and the class as God leads you. As long as it is blessing and life, trust that He is speaking through you!
- Carefully review the **During the Session: 3rd Meeting** section so you are prepared.
- Make sure any books/workbooks are ordered and bring them to class. If an administrator is doing this, check to make sure this is completed.
- Make sure that names and emails of any students desiring to join the closed *Marked by Love* community forum are emailed to admin@catherinetoon.com.
- Make sure that refreshments have been taken care of.
- Follow up with any students that are needing particular help.
- Prepare a list of contact information to be shared with the group (for people that agreed to share their information) – run off copies for the group, with extra for new students.
- Run off copies of the download for **Module 3: The Flavors of God**.
- Bring extra copies of **Module 1: Introduction**, and **Module 2: The Epicenter of the Universe** for new students.
- Run off/bring extra copies of *Personal Note from Catherine* for new people.

During the Meeting – 3rd Session

- Prayer/+ or - worship
- WELCOME everyone and introduce yourself and any leaders or administrators to any new students.
- Register new students – let them know that group information can be shared if permission is given:
  This can be anything from passing a sheet around to a formal registration process at your organization.
  I recommend getting at least:

    - full names
    - phone numbers
    - emails
    - permission to share those within the group, if desired (not everyone has to share), so that people can support one another and pray outside the meeting

- As you do this, get to know any new people. Ask new people to briefly share who they are, what they want from the class. Welcome them warmly.
- Do an ICE BREAKER to get people comfortable and to get to know one another. The goal is to laugh! Ha Ha Ha - If it's not fun, just say "no"! Choose from the list in the back of this guide or make up your own.
- Get your new student registration sheet back and make sure all new students have filled it out.
- Distribute any materials:

    - Downloadable workbook pdf for **Module 3 – The Flavors of God** – if for some reason you run out, email people a copy.
    - Pass out extra copies of workbook pdf **Module 1: Introduction, Module 2: The Epicenter of the Universe** for new students.
    - Make *sure* you give new people the *Personal Note from Catherine*.
    - Pass out Group Contact Information Sheet.

- Tell them that they will be watching the video for **Module 3** today.
- Remind them of the expectation that they go through the workbook for **Module 3** *before* the next meeting *on their own*. This is where the *real impact* of the course will happen as they encounter Love for themselves!
- Emphasize this is not homework as much as it is a time to receive ministry directly from the Lord.
- Urge them to plan now when they will start it and put it on their calendar. Give them a few minutes to look at their schedule and think about this.
- Tell new people to read through the *Personal Note from Catherine*. Explain that this course is designed to be loving, supportive, and safe. However, this is not a support group, nor does it replace counseling or other forms of help. During the week, we encourage people to pray for one another, but this also does not replace professional help and appropriate boundaries need to be maintained. Remind everyone to come see you if there are issues they need help with and you will do your best to help or connect them with help.
- Remind the group, that the *Marked by Love* environment needs to be safe for people to authentically share. That means **total confidentiality** unless there is harm to self or others at stake. What is said in class stays in class. No gossiping in the name of prayer chains!
- Have everyone stand up. Lead them in the **Remove the Mask Exercise.**
- Take any orders with monies for new:

    o softcover *Marked by Love* workbooks (if desired)
    o *Marked by Love* books (if desired)

Note: You can also have anyone order their own copies of either the softcover *Marked by Love* workbook or the *Marked by Love* book directly from Amazon or on my website https://catherinetoon.com.

- Remind them that they can have access to an optional *Marked by Love* Closed Community forum on Facebook just for *Marked by Love* students/leaders. Here, they'll be able to share and have fun connecting with their new global *Marked by Love* family. They will also be able to support one

another, if issues arise. Catherine will be ministering live and sharing other content intermittently via this venue.
- Pass around the registration form again so that people can circle their names if they are interested in checking it out.
- After class you should email us at: **admin@catherinetoon.com** providing us with the names and emails of any new students desiring to participate. We will promptly send them all the information they need and will approve their request, when they submit it to us.

General Discussion – facilitated by you, encouraging all students to share and no one to dominate the conversation:

- Ask students to share if they have struggled in the past or are currently struggling to find meaning in their lives.

    o Raise your hand if you can honestly say this has been a struggle.
    o Point out how common an issue this is for people (look around at all the raised hands).

- Ask how many of them have struggled to connect with God to be filled with His love.

    o Raise your hand if you can honestly say this has been a struggle.
    o Point out how common an issue this is for people (look around at all the raised hands).

- Ask students how they ranked themselves with ease of connecting with God scale of 1 – 10? You can have them raise their hands for each number.

    1 = I don't know God at all
    3 = I didn't know I could have a romance with God
    5 = between you and me, I am so bored with the whole God thing
    7 = sometimes I feel Him and sometimes I get distracted

8 = I can usually connect with God and feel I have a strong relationship with Him.
10 = I am wildly smitten and can't contain myself

- Share your experience briefly if you have had some victory here: "I used to be a '1' and now I am a '7' – I still struggle with ___, but God is helping me."

- Ask them if anyone has ever felt judged as being "out" of the approved body of Christ. Open that up for discussion.
- Ask them if anyone has ever fallen under the idea of people being in or out of the approved body of Christ. Was it a surprise that God is an inclusive God and invites the entire world to participate in intimate relationship with Him? Open that up for discussion.
- Ask if anyone wants to share about how Love has specifically made His mark on them.
- Give a 5-min. stretch/bathroom break.
- VIEW VIDEO - **Module 3: The Flavors of God** (approximately 39 min.).
- Allow people to ask questions and give short prayer requests.
- Close in prayer/give time for socializing if desired.

CONGRATULATIONS YOU COMPLETED THE THIRD MEETING!!

After the Meeting – 3rd Session

- Gather your new sign-up sheets
- Answer questions

MODULE 4

Who Am I?

God is love. By this the love of God was in us, that God has sent His only begotten Son into the world so that we might live through Him.
1 John 4:8-9 (NASB)

Goals of the Meeting – 4th Session

Administrative Goals:

- Distribute any materials
- Take any new orders (workbooks/books) & collect monies if needed (workbooks/book/ babysitting/refreshment fees)
  After class: promptly order workbooks/books and fulfill orders
- Update any preferences to join the *Marked by Love* closed Facebook forum
  After class: turn in information to admin@catherinetoon.com for those interested in joining the community

Ministry Goals:

- WELCOME EVERYONE
- Prayer/+ or – worship
- Get to know one another more – Ice Breaker/Remove the mask exercise
- General Discussion: **Module 3: The Flavors of God**
- View video: **Module 4: Who Am I?** (58 min.)
- Close in prayer/socializing if desired

Before the Meeting – 4th Session

- Watch video and complete all of **Module 4 – Who Am I?** in *Marked by Love* Workbook.
- Review *Marked by Love* Book **Chapter 3 – Who Am I?** (strongly suggested).

- Enjoy receiving and interacting on the closed *Marked by Love* community forum – this is YOUR course too!
- Pray for wisdom, guidance and inspiration as you lead; be open to any words from the Lord to share with the class. He always has something delightful to say.
- Pray for each student by name – speak over them and the class as God leads you. As long as it is blessing and life, trust that He is speaking through you!
- Carefully review the **During the Session: 4th Meeting** section so you are prepared.
- Make sure any books/workbooks are ordered and bring them to class. If an administrator is doing this, check to make sure this is completed.
- Make sure that names and emails of any students desiring to join the closed *Marked by Love* community forum are emailed to admin@catherinetoon.com.
- Make sure that refreshments have been taken care of.
- Follow up with any students that are needing particular help.
- Prepare a list of contact information to be shared with the group (for people that agreed to share their information) – run off copies for the group, with extra for new students.
- Run off copies of the download for **Module 4: Who Am I?** (make sure you have extra for new students).
- Bring extra copies of **Module 3: The Flavors of God** for those who were absent the previous week.

During the Meeting – 4th Session

- Prayer/+ or - worship
- Do your weekly ICE BREAKER.
- Distribute any materials:

  - Downloadable workbook pdf for **Module 4: Who Am I?** – if for some reason you run out, email people a copy.

- Pass out extra copies of workbook pdf **Module 3: The Flavors of God** for anyone who was absent last week.

- Tell them that they will be watching the video for **Module 4** today.
- Remind them of the expectation that they go through the workbook for **Module 4** *before* the next meeting *on their own*. This is where the *real impact* of the course will happen as they encounter Love for themselves!
- Emphasize this is not homework as much as it is a time to receive ministry directly from the Lord.
- Urge them to plan now when they will start it and put it on their calendar. Give them a few minutes to look at their schedule and think about this.
- Have everyone stand up and lead them in the **Remove the Mask Exercise.**
- Take any orders with monies for new:

  - softcover *Marked by Love* workbooks (if desired)
  - *Marked by Love* books (if desired)

Note: You can also have anyone order their own copies of either the softcover *Marked by Love* workbook or the *Marked by Love* book directly from Amazon or on my website https://catherinetoon.com.

- Remind them that they can still join the *Marked by Love* Closed Community forum on Facebook just for *Marked by Love* students/leaders.
- Pass around the registration form again so that people can circle their names if they are interested in checking it out.
- After class you should email us at: **admin@catherinetoon.com** providing us with the names and emails of any new students desiring to participate. We will promptly send them all the information they need and will approve their request, when they submit it to us.

General Discussion – facilitated by you, encouraging all students to share and no one to dominate the conversation. **Note**: this video is 58 min. (19 min.

longer than the Session 3 video), so you will want to adjust your discussion time/other time accordingly:

- Ask students to share if they have struggled with misconceptions of God. What has that looked like?
- Ask them to pinpoint if they have conflicted feelings about God. Have them raise their hands for these common conflicts:

  - Angry — Forgiving
  - Disappointed — Helping
  - Wimpy — Peaceful
  - Disinterested — Powerful
  - Distant — Good
  - Changeable — Merciful
  - Corrects with trials — Teaching
  - Scary — Big

- Ask them how God has not looked or felt like love for them (these are lies that feel like truth) and what Love showed them
- Give a 5-min. stretch/bathroom break.
- VIEW VIDEO - **Module 4: Who Am I?** (approximately 58 min.).
- Allow people to ask questions and give short prayer requests.
- Close in prayer/give time for socializing if desired.

CONGRATULATIONS YOU COMPLETED THE FOURTH MEETING!!

After the Meeting - 4th Session

- Gather your new sign-up sheets
- Answer questions

MODULE 5

What's Wrong?

God is love. By this the love of God was in us, that God has sent His only begotten Son into the world so that we might live through Him.
1 John 4:8-9 (NASB)

Goals of the Meeting – 5th Session

Administrative Goals:

- Distribute any materials
- Take any new orders (workbooks/books) & collect monies if needed (workbooks/book/ babysitting/refreshment fees)
  After class: promptly order workbooks/books and fulfill orders
- Update any preferences to join the *Marked by Love* closed Facebook forum
  After class: turn in information to admin@catherinetoon.com for those interested in joining the community

Ministry Goals:

- WELCOME EVERYONE
- Prayer/+ or - worship
- Get to know one another more – Ice Breaker/Remove the mask exercise
- View Video: **Module 5: What's Wrong?** (40 min.)
- General Discussion
- Close in prayer/socializing if desired

Before the Meeting – 5th Session

- Watch video and complete all of **Module 5 – What's Wrong?** in *Marked by Love* Workbook.
- Review *Marked by Love* Book **Chapter 4 – What's Wrong?** (strongly suggested).

- Enjoy receiving and interacting on the closed *Marked by Love* community forum – this is YOUR course too!
- Pray for wisdom, guidance and inspiration as you lead; be open to any words from the Lord to share with the class. He always has something delightful to say.
- Pray for each student by name – speak over them and the class as God leads you. As long as it is blessing and life, trust that He is speaking through you!
- Carefully review the **During the Session: 5th Meeting** section so you are prepared.
- Make sure any books/workbooks are ordered and bring them to class. If an administrator is doing this, check to make sure this is completed.
- Make sure that names and emails of any students desiring to join the closed *Marked by Love* community forum are emailed to admin@catherinetoon.com.
- Make sure that refreshments have been taken care of.
- Follow up with any students that are needing particular help.
- Prepare a list of contact information to be shared with the group (for people that agreed to share their information) – run off copies for the group, with extra for new students.
- Run off copies of the download for **Module 5: What's Wrong?** (make sure you have extra for new students).
- Bring extra copies of **Module 4: Who Am I?** for those who were absent the previous week.

During the Meeting – 5th Session

- Prayer/+ or - worship
- Do your weekly ICE BREAKER.
- Distribute any materials:

    - Downloadable workbook pdf for **Module 5: What's Wrong?** – if for some reason you run out, email people a copy.

- Pass out extra copies of workbook pdf **Module 4: Who Am I?** for anyone who was absent last week.

- Tell them that they will be watching the video for **Module 5** today.
- Remind them of the expectation that they go through the workbook for **Module 5** *before* the next meeting *on their own*. This is where the *real impact* of the course will happen as they encounter Love for themselves!
- Emphasize this is not homework as much as it is a time to receive ministry directly from the Lord.
- Urge them to plan now when they will start it and put it on their calendar. Give them a few minutes to look at their schedule and think about this.
- Have everyone stand up and lead them in the **Remove the Mask Exercise.**
- Take any orders with monies for new:

  - softcover *Marked by Love* workbooks (if desired)
  - *Marked by Love* books (if desired)

Note: You can also have anyone order their own copies of either the softcover *Marked by Love* workbook or the *Marked by Love* book directly from Amazon or on my website https://catherinetoon.com.

- Remind them that they can still join the *Marked by Love* Closed Community forum on Facebook just for *Marked by Love* students/leaders.
- Pass around the registration form again so that people can circle their names if they are interested in checking it out.
- After class you should email us at: **admin@catherinetoon.com** providing us with the names and emails of any new students desiring to participate. We will promptly send them all the information they need and will approve their request, when they submit it to us.

General Discussion – facilitated by you, encouraging all students to share and no one to dominate the conversation. **Note**: this video is 40 min:

- Ask students to share if they have struggled with who they are and what that looked like.
- Ask them how hard it was to connect with the truth that they are Love's poem/His masterpiece. Ask them to share.
- Ask them how much they struggle with defining themselves by what they do (performance)?
- Ask them to share their encounters with Love – one with Him, Him in them and them in Him.
- Give a 5-min. stretch/bathroom break.
- VIEW VIDEO - **Module 5: What's Wrong?** (approximately 40 min.).
- Allow people to ask questions and give short prayer requests.
- Close in prayer/give time for socializing if desired.

CONGRATULATIONS YOU COMPLETED THE FIFTH MEETING!!

After the Meeting – 5th Session

- Gather your new sign-up sheets
- Answer questions

MODULE 6

What's Right?

God is love. By this the love of God was in us, that God has sent His only begotten Son into the world so that we might live through Him.
1 John 4:8-9 (NASB)

Goals of the Meeting – 6th Session

Administrative Goals:

- Distribute any materials
- Take any new orders (workbooks/books) & collect monies if needed (workbooks/book/ babysitting/refreshment fees)
  After class: promptly order workbooks/books and fulfill orders
- Update any preferences to join the *Marked by Love* closed Facebook forum
  After class: turn in information to admin@catherinetoon.com for those interested in joining the community

Ministry Goals:

- WELCOME EVERYONE
- Prayer/+ or - worship
- Get to know one another more – Ice Breaker/Remove the mask exercise
- View Video: **Module 6: What's Right?** (24 min.)
- General Discussion
- Close in prayer/socializing if desired

Before the Meeting – 6th Session

- Watch video and complete all of **Module 6 – What's Right?** in *Marked by Love* Workbook.
- Review *Marked by Love* Book **Chapter 5 – What's Right?** (strongly suggested).

- Enjoy receiving and interacting on the closed *Marked by Love* community forum – this is YOUR course too!
- Pray for wisdom, guidance and inspiration as you lead; be open to any words from the Lord to share with the class. He always has something delightful to say.
- Pray for each student by name – speak over them and the class as God leads you. As long as it is blessing and life, trust that He is speaking through you!
- Carefully review the **During the Session: 6th Meeting** section so you are prepared.
- Make sure any books/workbooks are ordered and bring them to class. If an administrator is doing this, check to make sure this is completed.
- Make sure that names and emails of any students desiring to join the closed *Marked by Love* community forum are emailed to admin@catherinetoon.com.
- Make sure that refreshments have been taken care of.
- Follow up with any students that are needing particular help.
- Prepare a list of contact information to be shared with the group (for people that agreed to share their information) – run off copies for the group, with extra for new students.
- Run off copies of the download for **Module 6: What's Right?** (make sure you have extra for new students).
- Bring extra copies of **Module 5: What's Wrong?** for those who were absent the previous week.

During the Meeting – 6th Session

- Prayer/+ or - worship
- Do your weekly ICE BREAKER.
- Distribute any materials:

    - Downloadable workbook pdf for **Module 6: What's Right?** – if for some reason you run out, email people a copy.

- Pass out extra copies of workbook pdf **Module 5: What's Wrong?** for anyone who was absent last week.

- Tell them that they will be watching the video for **Module 6** today.
- Remind them of the expectation that they go through the workbook for **Module 6** *before* the next meeting *on their own*. This is where the *real impact* of the course will happen as they encounter Love for themselves!
- Emphasize this is not homework as much as it is a time to receive ministry directly from the Lord.
- Urge them to plan now when they will start it and put it on their calendar. Give them a few minutes to look at their schedule and think about this.
- Have everyone stand up and lead them in the **Remove the Mask Exercise.**
- Take any orders with monies for new:

  - softcover *Marked by Love* workbooks (if desired)
  - *Marked by Love* books (if desired)

Note: You can also have anyone order their own copies of either the softcover *Marked by Love* workbook or the *Marked by Love* book directly from Amazon or on my website https://catherinetoon.com.

- Remind them that they can still join the *Marked by Love* Closed Community forum on Facebook just for *Marked by Love* students/leaders.
- Pass around the registration form again so that people can circle their names if they are interested in checking it out.
- After class you should email us at: **admin@catherinetoon.com** providing us with the names and emails of any new students desiring to participate. We will promptly send them all the information they need and will approve their request, when they submit it to us.

General Discussion – facilitated by you, encouraging all students to share and no one to dominate the conversation. **Note:** this video is 24 min., so you have extra time for sharing or prayer requests.

- Ask students how much they struggle seeing themselves or others as problems.
- Ask how hard is it for them to connect with the scriptural truth that their "old man" / "sin nature" was really crucified/killed off, it does not resurrect, and that they are totally a "new creation".
- How well do you connect with the fact that you were made Christ's righteousness?
- How many have felt brainwashed that there is something wrong with them or that they are guilty and condemnable?
- Ask them to share what they got about the truth of who they are, created in Love, holy and blameless before the foundation of the world.
- Give a 5-min. stretch/bathroom break.
- VIEW VIDEO - **Module 6: What's Right**? (approximately 24 min.).
- Allow people to ask questions and give short prayer requests.
- Close in prayer/give time for socializing if desired.

CONGRATULATIONS YOU COMPLETED THE SIXTH MEETING!!

After the Meeting - 6th Session

- Gather your new sign-up sheets
- Answer questions

MODULE 7

The Object of God's Passion

God is love. By this the love of God was in us, that God has sent His only begotten Son into the world so that we might live through Him.
1 John 4:8-9 (NASB)

Goals of the Meeting – 7th Session

Administrative Goals:

- Distribute any materials
- Take any new orders (workbooks/books) & collect monies if needed (workbooks/book/ babysitting/refreshment fees)
  After class: promptly order workbooks/books and fulfill orders
- Update any preferences to join the *Marked by Love* closed Facebook forum
  After class: turn in information to admin@catherinetoon.com for those interested in joining the community

Ministry Goals:

- WELCOME EVERYONE
- Prayer/+ or - worship
- Get to know one another more – Ice Breaker/Remove the mask exercise
- General Discussion: **Module 6: What's Right?**
- View Video: **Module 7: The Object of God's Passion** (71 min)
- Close in prayer/socializing if desired

Before the Meeting – 7th Session

- Watch video and complete all of **Module 7 – The Object of God's Passion** in *Marked by Love* Workbook.
- Review *Marked by Love* Book **Chapter 6 – The Object of God's Passion** (strongly suggested).

- Enjoy receiving and interacting on the closed *Marked by Love* community forum – this is YOUR course too!
- Pray for wisdom, guidance and inspiration as you lead; be open to any words from the Lord to share with the class. He always has something delightful to say.
- Pray for each student by name – speak over them and the class as God leads you. As long as it is blessing and life, trust that He is speaking through you!
- Carefully review the **During the Session: 7th Meeting** section so you are prepared.
- Make sure any books/workbooks are ordered and bring them to class. If an administrator is doing this, check to make sure this is completed.
- Make sure that names and emails of any students desiring to join the closed *Marked by Love* community forum are emailed to admin@catherinetoon.com.
- Make sure that refreshments have been taken care of.
- Follow up with any students that are needing particular help.
- Prepare a list of contact information to be shared with the group (for people that agreed to share their information) – run off copies for the group, with extra for new students.
- Run off copies of the download for **Module 7: The Object of God's Passion** (make sure you have extra for new students).
- Bring extra copies of **Module 6: What's Right?** for those who were absent the previous week.

During the Meeting – 7th Session

- Prayer/+ or - worship
- Do your weekly ICE BREAKER.
- Distribute any materials:

    - Downloadable workbook pdf for **Module 7: The Object of God's Passion** – if for some reason you run out, email people a copy.

- Pass out extra copies of workbook pdf **Module 6: What's Right?** for anyone who was absent last week.

- Tell them that they will be watching the video for **Module 7** today.
- Remind them of the expectation that they go through the workbook for **Module 7** *before* the next meeting *on their own*. This is where the *real impact* of the course will happen as they encounter Love for themselves!
- Emphasize this is not homework as much as it is a time to receive ministry directly from the Lord.
- Urge them to plan now when they will start it and put it on their calendar. Give them a few minutes to look at their schedule and think about this.
- Have everyone stand up and lead them in the **Remove the Mask Exercise.**
- Take any orders with monies for new:

  - softcover *Marked by Love* workbooks (if desired)
  - *Marked by Love* books (if desired)

Note: You can also have anyone order their own copies of either the softcover *Marked by Love* workbook or the *Marked by Love* book directly from Amazon or on my website https://catherinetoon.com.

- Remind them that they can still join the *Marked by Love* Closed Community forum on Facebook just for *Marked by Love* students/leaders.
- Pass around the registration form again so that people can circle their names if they are interested in checking it out.
- After class you should email us at:
- **admin@catherinetoon.com** providing us with the names and emails of any new students desiring to participate. We will promptly send them all the information they need and will approve their request, when they submit it to us.

General Discussion – facilitated by you, encouraging all students to share and no one to dominate the conversation. **Note**: this video is 71 min, so you will have to limit discussion and prayer time accordingly.

- Ask students how much they have struggled with feeling like they have to earn their own righteousness in some way. What does that look like?
- Ask how God showed them that they have been created as a solution and a champion for Love.
- Give a 5-min. stretch/bathroom break.
- VIEW VIDEO - **Module 7: The Object of God's Passion** (approximately 71 min.).
- Allow people to ask questions and give short prayer requests.
- Close in prayer/give time for socializing if desired.

CONGRATULATIONS YOU COMPLETED THE SEVENTH MEETING!!

After the Meeting – 7ᵗʰ Session

- Answer questions

MODULE 8

Getting There from Here – Finishing at the Starting Point

God is love. By this the love of God was in us, that God has sent His only begotten Son into the world so that we might live through Him.
1 John 4:8-9 (NASB)

Goals of the Meeting – 8th Session

Administrative Goals:

- Distribute any materials
- Take any new orders (workbooks/books) & collect monies if needed (workbooks/book/ babysitting/refreshment fees)
  After class: promptly order workbooks/books and fulfill orders
- Update any preferences to join the *Marked by Love* closed Facebook forum
  After class: turn in information to admin@catherinetoon.com for those interested in joining the community

Ministry Goals:

- WELCOME EVERYONE
- Prayer/+ or - worship
- Get to know one another more – Ice Breaker/Remove the mask exercise
- General Discussion: **Module 7 Video: The Object of God's Passion**
- View Video: **Module 8: Getting There from Here - Finishing at the Starting Point** (14 min)
- Close in prayer/socializing if desired

Before the Meeting – 8th Session

- Watch video and complete all of **Module 8: – Getting There from Here - Finishing at the Starting Point** in *Marked by Love* Workbook.

- Review *Marked by Love* Book **Chapter 7 – Getting There from Here – Finishing at the Starting Point** (strongly suggested).
- Enjoy receiving and interacting on the closed *Marked by Love* community forum – this is YOUR course too!
- Pray for wisdom, guidance and inspiration as you lead; be open to any words from the Lord to share with the class. He always has something delightful to say.
- Pray for each student by name – speak over them and the class as God leads you. As long as it is blessing and life, trust that He is speaking through you!
- Carefully review the **During the Session: 8th Meeting** section so you are prepared.
- Make sure any books/workbooks are ordered and bring them to class. If an administrator is doing this, check to make sure this is completed.
- Make sure that names and emails of any students desiring to join the closed *Marked by Love* community forum are emailed to admin@catherinetoon.com.
- Make sure that refreshments have been taken care of.
- Follow up with any students that are needing particular help.
- Prepare a list of contact information to be shared with the group (for people that agreed to share their information) – run off copies for the group, with extra for new students.
- Run off copies of the download for **Module 8: Getting There from Here – Finishing at the Starting Point** (make sure you have extra for new students).
- Bring extra copies of **Module 7: The Object of God's Passion** for those who were absent the previous week.

During the Meeting – 8th Session

- Prayer/+ or - worship
- Do your weekly ICE BREAKER.
- Distribute any materials:

- Downloadable workbook pdf for **Module 8: Getting There from Here – Finishing at the Starting Point** – if for some reason you run out, email people a copy.
- Pass out extra copies of workbook pdf **Module 7: The Object of God's Passion** for anyone who was absent last week.

- Tell them that they will be watching the video for **Module 8** today.
- Remind them of the expectation that they go through the workbook for **Module 8** *before* the next meeting *on their own*. This is where the *real impact* of the course will happen as they encounter Love for themselves!
- Emphasize this is not homework as much as it is a time to receive ministry directly from the Lord.
- Urge them to plan now when they will start it and put it on their calendar. Give them a few minutes to look at their schedule and think about this.
- Have everyone stand up and lead them in the **Remove the Mask Exercise.**
- Take any orders with monies for new:

    - softcover *Marked by Love* workbooks (if desired)
    - *Marked by Love* books (if desired)

Note: You can also have anyone order their own copies of either the softcover *Marked by Love* workbook or the *Marked by Love* book directly from Amazon or on my website https://catherinetoon.com.

- Remind them that they can still join the *Marked by Love* Closed Community forum on Facebook just for *Marked by Love* students/leaders.
- Pass around the registration form again so that people can circle their names if they are interested in checking it out.
- After class you should email us at:
- **admin@catherinetoon.com** providing us with the names and emails of any new students desiring to participate. We will promptly send them all the information they need and will approve their request, when they submit it to us.

General Discussion – facilitated by you, encouraging all students to share and no one to dominate the conversation. *Note: this video is only 13 min., so you will have much more time for discussion and prayer, be sure to plan accordingly.*

- Ask the students how hard or easy it is it for them to connect to the delight of God over them.
- Ask how hard or easy is it for them to connect with depending upon Love like a little child. Ask them why.
- Ask how many students feel "behind schedule" in their lives.
- In the Prodigal Son story, ask which brother they can relate to more – the Prodigal or the Elder Brother.
- Ask them to share what Love revealed about the reasons they are on planet Earth.
- Ask them what Love revealed about the lies they believe about their life assignments and what truth He revealed.
- Give a 5-min. stretch/bathroom break.
- VIEW VIDEO - **Module 8: Getting There from Here – Finishing at the Starting Point** (approximately 13 min.).
- Allow people to ask questions and give prayer requests.
- Close in prayer/give time for socializing if desired.

CONGRATULATIONS YOU COMPLETED THE EIGHTH MEETING!!

After the Meeting – 8th Session

- Answer questions

MODULE 9

Freaky Rest

God is love. By this the love of God was in us, that God has sent His only begotten Son into the world so that we might live through Him.
1 John 4:8-9 (NASB)

Goals of the Meeting – 9th Session

Administrative Goals:

- Distribute any materials
- Take any new orders (workbooks/books) & collect monies if needed (workbooks/book/ babysitting/refreshment fees)
  After class: promptly order workbooks/books and fulfill orders
- Update any preferences to join the *Marked by Love* closed Facebook forum
  After class: turn in information to admin@catherinetoon.com for those interested in joining the community

Ministry Goals:

- WELCOME EVERYONE
- Prayer/+ or - worship
- Get to know one another more – Ice Breaker/Remove the mask exercise
- General Discussion: **Module 8: Getting There from Here – Finishing at the Starting Point**
- View Video: **Module 9: Freaky Rest** (37 min)
- Close in prayer/socializing if desired

Before the Meeting – 9th Session

- Watch video and complete all of **Module 9 – Freaky Rest** in *Marked by Love* Workbook.

- Review *Marked by Love* Book **Chapter 8 – Freaky Rest** (strongly suggested).
- Enjoy receiving and interacting on the closed *Marked by Love* community forum – this is YOUR course too!
- Pray for wisdom, guidance and inspiration as you lead; be open to any words from the Lord to share with the class. He always has something delightful to say.
- Pray for each student by name – speak over them and the class as God leads you. As long as it is blessing and life, trust that He is speaking through you!
- Carefully review the **During the Session: 9th Meeting** section so you are prepared.
- Make sure any books/workbooks are ordered and bring them to class. If an administrator is doing this, check to make sure this is completed.
- Make sure that names and emails of any students desiring to join the closed *Marked by Love* community forum are emailed to admin@catherinetoon.com.
- Make sure that refreshments have been taken care of.
- Follow up with any students that are needing particular help.
- Prepare a list of contact information to be shared with the group (for people that agreed to share their information) – run off copies for the group, with extra for new students.
- Run off copies of the download for **Module 9: Freaky Rest** (make sure you have extra for new students).
- Bring extra copies of **Module 8: Getting There from Here – Finishing at the Starting Point** for those who were absent the previous week.

During the Meeting – 9th Session

- Prayer/+ or - worship
- Do your weekly ICE BREAKER.
- Distribute any materials:

- Downloadable workbook pdf for **Module 9: Freaky Rest** – if for some reason you run out, email people a copy.
- Pass out extra copies of workbook pdf **Module 8: Getting There from Here – Finishing at the Starting Point** for anyone who was absent last week.

- Tell them that they will be watching the video for **Module 9** today.
- Remind them of the expectation that they go through the workbook for **Module 9** *before* the next meeting *on their own*. This is where the *real impact* of the course will happen as they encounter Love for themselves!
- Emphasize this is not homework as much as it is a time to receive ministry directly from the Lord.
- Urge them to plan now when they will start it and put it on their calendar. Give them a few minutes to look at their schedule and think about this.
- Have everyone stand up and lead them in the **Remove the Mask Exercise.**
- Take any orders with monies for new:

  - softcover *Marked by Love* workbooks (if desired)
  - *Marked by Love* books (if desired)

Note: You can also have anyone order their own copies of either the softcover *Marked by Love* workbook or the *Marked by Love* book directly from Amazon or on my website https://catherinetoon.com.

- Remind them that they can still join the *Marked by Love* Closed Community forum on Facebook just for *Marked by Love* students/leaders.
- Pass around the registration form again so that people can circle their names if they are interested in checking it out.
- After class you should email us at:
- **admin@catherinetoon.com** providing us with the names and emails of any new students desiring to participate. We will promptly send them all the information they need and will approve their request, when they submit it to us.

General Discussion – facilitated by you, encouraging all students to share and no one to dominate the conversation. This video is 37 min.

- Ask students if they can relate to the truth that they can relax because they are in Christ. How true does that feel?
- Ask if it was surprising to see God as relaxed.
- Ask if they can share how Love covers them and the details of their lives. Have them share if that has been a struggle.
- What did Love reveal there?
- Give a 5-min. stretch/bathroom break.
- VIEW VIDEO - **Module 9: Freaky Rest** (approximately 37 min.).
- Allow people to ask questions and give prayer requests.
- Close in prayer/give time for socializing if desired.

CONGRATULATIONS YOU COMPLETED THE NINTH MEETING!!

After the Meeting – 9th Session

- Answer questions

MODULE 10

Your Love Story

God is love. By this the love of God was in us, that God has sent His only begotten Son into the world so that we might live through Him.
1 John 4:8-9 (NASB)

Goals of the Meeting – 10th Session

Administrative Goals:

- Distribute any materials
- Take any new orders (workbooks/books) & collect monies if needed (workbooks/book/ babysitting/refreshment fees)
  After class: promptly order workbooks/books and fulfill orders
- Update any preferences to join the *Marked by Love* closed Facebook forum
  After class: turn in information to admin@catherinetoon.com for those interested in joining the community

Ministry Goals:

- WELCOME EVERYONE
- Prayer/+ or - worship
- Get to know one another more – Ice Breaker/Remove the mask exercise
- General Discussion: **Module 9: Freaky Rest**
- View Video: **Module 10: Your Love Story** (38 min)
- Close in prayer/socializing if desired

Before the Meeting – 10th Session

- Watch video and complete all of **Module 10 – Your Love Story** in *Marked by Love* Workbook.
- Review *Marked by Love* Book **Chapter 9 – True Confessions** (strongly suggested).

- Enjoy receiving and interacting on the closed *Marked by Love* community forum – this is YOUR course too!
- Pray for wisdom, guidance and inspiration as you lead; be open to any words from the Lord to share with the class. He always has something delightful to say.
- Pray for each student by name – speak over them and the class as God leads you. As long as it is blessing and life, trust that He is speaking through you!
- Carefully review the **During the Session: 10th Meeting** section so you are prepared.
- Make sure any books/workbooks are ordered and bring them to class. If an administrator is doing this, check to make sure this is completed.
- Make sure that names and emails of any students desiring to join the closed *Marked by Love* community forum are emailed to admin@catherinetoon.com.
- Make sure that refreshments have been taken care of.
- Follow up with any students that are needing particular help.
- Prepare a list of contact information to be shared with the group (for people that agreed to share their information) – run off copies for the group, with extra for new students.
- Run off copies of the download for **Module 10: Your Love Story** (make sure you have extra for new students).
- Bring extra copies of **Module 9: Freaky Rest** for those who were absent the previous week.

During the Meeting – 10th Session

- Prayer/+ or - worship
- Do your weekly ICE BREAKER.
- Distribute any materials:

    - Downloadable workbook pdf for **Module 10: Your Love Story** – if for some reason you run out, email people a copy.

- Pass out extra copies of workbook pdf **Module 9: Freaky Rest** for anyone who was absent last week.

- Tell them that they will be watching the video for **Module 10** today.
- Remind them of the expectation that they go through the workbook for **Module 10** *before* the next meeting *on their own*. This is where the *real impact* of the course will happen as they encounter Love for themselves!
- Emphasize this is not homework as much as it is a time to receive ministry directly from the Lord.
- Urge them to plan now when they will start it and put it on their calendar. Give them a few minutes to look at their schedule and think about this.
- Have everyone stand up and lead them in the **Remove the Mask Exercise.**
- Take any orders with monies for new:

  - softcover *Marked by Love* workbooks (if desired)
  - *Marked by Love* books (if desired)

  Note: You can also have anyone order their own copies of either the softcover *Marked by Love* workbook or the *Marked by Love* book directly from Amazon or on my website https://catherinetoon.com.

- Remind them that they can still join the *Marked by Love* Closed Community forum on Facebook just for *Marked by Love* students/leaders.
- Pass around the registration form again so that people can circle their names if they are interested in checking it out.
- After class you should email us at:
- **admin@catherinetoon.com** providing us with the names and emails of any new students desiring to participate. We will promptly send them all the information they need and will approve their request, when they submit it to us.

General Discussion – facilitated by you, encouraging all students to share and no one to dominate the conversation. This video is 38 min.

- We have been translated from the kingdom of darkness into the kingdom of light (Colossians 1:13). Ask how challenging that is for the students to believe. For those that say they struggle to believe that, explain that it is because of one of the following reasons:

    - they haven't been taught that truth
    - they have forgotten that truth, or
    - they don't recognize that truth operating in their lives

- Have students share the areas that cause them to get out of rest and be at peace: Have them share: what the lies are that they are believing about those areas?
- Have them share truths Love gave them about those areas.
- Give a 5-min. stretch/bathroom break.
- VIEW LAST VIDEO: **Module 10: Your Love Story** (approximately 38 min.).
- Allow people to ask questions and give prayer requests.
- Close in prayer/give time for socializing if desired.

CONGRATULATIONS YOU COMPLETED THE TENTH MEETING!! ONE MORE MEETING TO GO!!!

After the Meeting – 10th Session

- Answer questions

MODULE 11

Follow Up: Your Love Story – 11th Meeting

*God is love. By this the love of God was in us, that God has sent His only
begotten Son into the world so that we might live through Him.*
1 John 4:8-9 (NASB)

Goals of the Meeting – 11th Session

Administrative Goals:

- Remind the students about the *Marked by Love* closed Facebook forum & let them know they can still join and participate even after the class ends.
After class: turn in information to admin@catherinetoon.com for those interested in joining the community

Ministry Goals:

- WELCOME EVERYONE – This is the last class!
- Prayer/+ or - worship
- Last Ice Breaker/Remove the Mask exercise
- General Discussion: **Module 10: Your Love Story**
- No video
- Close in prayer/socializing if desired

Before the Meeting – 11th Session

- Review and reflect on **Module 10: Your Love Story** in the *Marked by Love* Workbook.
- Review the *Marked by Love* Book **Chapter 9: True Confessions**, if desired.
- Enjoy receiving and interacting on the closed *Marked by Love* community forum – this is YOUR course too!

- Pray for wisdom, guidance and inspiration as you finish up the course; see if the Lord will give you a word to share with the class.
- Pray for each student by name – speak over them and the class whatever as God leads you. As long as it is blessing and life, trust that He is speaking through you!
- Carefully review the **During the Session: 11th Meeting** so you are prepared.
- Make sure any final books/workbook are ordered and bring them to class. If an administrator is doing this, check to make sure this is completed.
- Make sure that names and emails of any students desiring to join the closed *Marked by Love* community forum are emailed to admin@catherinetoon.com.
- Make sure that refreshments have been taken care of.
- Follow up with any students that are needing particular help.

During the Meeting – 11th Session

- Prayer/+ or - worship
- WELCOME everyone to their last class.
- Do your last weekly ICE BREAKER.
- Tell the class that this will be discussion and prayer only. There is no video today.
- Have everyone stand up. Lead them in their final **Remove the Mask Exercise.**
- Refer any students who are interested to order the *Marked by Love* workbook or book directly from Amazon or through my website at: catherinetoon.com.
- Remind them that they can have access to an optional *Marked by Love* Closed Community forum on Facebook just for *Marked by Love* students/leaders. They can continue to be a part of this community even after they finish the course.

General Discussion – facilitated by you, encouraging all students to share and no one to dominate the conversation. There is no video.

- Ask students to share what Love was doing and how He made His mark on them during:

  · Womb/Birth/Early Childhood
  · Late Childhood/Early Teens
  · Late Teens/Early Adulthood
  · Adulthood: 20's
  · Adulthood: 30's
  · Adulthood: 40's
  · Adulthood: 50's
  · Adulthood: 60's
  · Adulthood: 70's and Beyond
  · What did Love reveal about where they are now and where they are headed?

Encourage them to periodically revisit the Love Encounter Breaks during different seasons of their lives to glean even more.

- Give a 5-min. stretch/bathroom break as needed.
- Allow people to ask questions and give prayer requests.
- Close in prayer, blessing the students to continue to spend time intentionally encountering Love.
- Give time for socializing if desired.

CONGRATULATIONS YOU COMPLETED THE ENTIRE *MARKED BY LOVE* COURSE!!! THANK YOU FOR BEING AN INSTRUMENT TO CONNECT PEOPLE WITH LOVE!!!

After the Meeting – 11th Session

- Answer questions and pray with individuals

A Personal Note from Catherine

Hello There!

I am so excited that you have signed up for the *Marked by Love* Course in your group!

God is Love and has such amazing things for you! He wants to reveal those things to you intimately and specifically where you are right now. Intermittently, I briefly share things in my *Marked by Love* series that have happened in my past that were traumatic and deeply wounding. Many of you have suffered or are suffering in very deep ways. I would be doing you a disservice if I didn't outline what you can expect from your *Marked by Love* course and what is not appropriate to expect. Different types of ministry are designed for different situations.

The *Marked by Love* course is designed to help you connect directly to God, Who is the ultimate Source of everything you need. In the context of a small group, there is definite ministry to one another – support, celebration, and inspiration. People need people, but it is crucial to understand that no one, not even your spouse or closest friend is the Source – they are a conduit. When we make people our source, we end up draining them and feeling disillusioned and empty ourselves because only God is limitless Love. In that, we still are designed to need people and be *inter-dependent*.

The roles people play are designed to be different. A small group gives support, but is not designed as an in-depth support group or counseling. While friendships will form, these take time. It is wise to let God choose to deepen the ties moving from acquaintance to friendship to an inner circle friend that is based on more than meeting needs. Keeping God as the ultimate Source will protect you from developing co-dependencies that are not healthy or helpful.

The need to connect with God, know Him more, receive freedom through Him, know who you are as a son/daughter, and know your purpose, are universal. We all come from different backgrounds and find ourselves in different specific places. We all will find ourselves with different needs specific to us when we go through any course, including this one. Support groups, counseling, inner healing ministry, spiritual mentoring/interventions, medical interventions (traditional or nontraditional), all have a place for meeting needs that are specific to us. Abuse, tragedy, addictions, relational challenges, loss, spiritual challenges and all the things that we can face as human beings in a fallen world, require specific help. While the *Marked by Love* course and your group/small group will interlace with what you need for healing, deliverance, wise counsel, therapy, and/or emotional support, if you are going through a significant challenge, you will need more than what this course provides, or than what your group and group facilitator can or should offer.

Although your emotional/spiritual/physical needs are totally valid, it is important that the group stay focused on the course as it is laid out and your meeting not become a forum that gets off target to focus overly on any one person's specific situation. Whatever help you need outside of the constructs of the course, for your sake and those who love you, be proactive in getting it! You are worth whatever it takes to get the help you need! The course, your facilitator, or small group members should not be the only conduit for help in serious situations. God is masterful at leading and providing for you to get what you need definitively, while gleaning from the course and the people in it.

Your needs and the needs of others are totally valid and important. There are proper places to have those needs met and, in every case, boundaries are super important to keep everyone healthy, including you! Ask God what intimate details of your life are appropriate to share, and how much, if this is new to you. He will totally help you! We want this to be a safe place for everyone.

Oversharing will put you in a vulnerable position, hijack the purposes of the course, possibly trigger others who really are not a in a position to handle it, as well as, put responsibilities on the group that are not appropriate. With that, under-sharing will make the group superficial, stuck in conceptual facts, and hinder the impacting of hearts and lives.

There is a glorious balance that will bring life to both you and the group. So, by all means, share, just share appropriately. Allow people to give you feedback if you don't know what that looks like. And, of course, Holy Spirit will totally help you! Remember He's the Helper, He's masterful, and He loves His job. But mostly, He's wild about you and your freedom!

I am totally trusting Him on your behalf to have this course be everything He intended it to be for you and your group. I am also trusting Him with everything you need right where you are! He is masterful because He is Love and Love never fails!

Much love,
Catherine

P.S. Here are some tips for completing the workbook exercises:

- Stay current with each week, at least partially
- Finishing each week is a priority, if you are getting more in a particular exercise, come back to it later so you can finish the week and won't get bogged down
- Skip over exercises that you are struggling with and come back to them later
- Remember that everyone can come back and redo the exercises as situations change – the Lord ALWAYS has more to say! This is not a one-shot deal!
- Be honest with yourself about how much time the workbook will take. This is more about luxuriating in the truths Love is giving you, not checking off your exercise list. This is worth adequate time!
- Don't wait until the night before the next meeting to start. This will keep you from stressing. If you are more of a last-minute person, you may want to make your deadline 2 nights before the session (kind of like setting your clock 15 minutes before you want to get up, knowing you will hit the snooze button). This will help you - you can do this!

Icebreaker Games and Activities

The M&M Game

Fill a bowl with M&Ms and pass around the group. Ask each person to take a *small* handful of M&Ms. Once the bowl of M&Ms has been passed around, explain the colors of the M&Ms mean certain things, such as:

>   **Red:** Favorite superhero
>   **Orange:** Favorite outdoor activity
>   **Blue:** Favorite food
>   **Green:** Favorite vacation spot
>   **Brown:** Favorite TV show
>   **Yellow:** Favorite thing to do in your free time

Then circle around the table and ask your team to give answers for the M&Ms they scooped out of the bowl.

Desert Island

If you were trapped on a desert island with only one comfort item, no matter how big or ridiculous, what would that be?

Year of the Coin

Hand out a coin to each person and ask people to share something they were doing the year the coin was minted. Be sure to sift through the coins beforehand to make sure your team was born when the coins were minted though.

2 Truths and a Lie

Have everyone in the group write down 3 statements about themselves. 2 need to be true, and 1 needs to be a lie. Have everyone take turns reading their statements, and the other members of the group need to come to a consensus about which statement is a lie.

Paper Airplane Game

Pass out a sheet a paper to each person attending the meeting. Then ask everyone to write an interesting fact about themselves on the piece of paper and fold it into a paper airplane. Everyone should then launch their paper airplane to somewhere around the room. Each person then grabs a launched paper airplane and guesses who the interesting fact belongs to.

Marooned

Go around the table and ask each person, "If you were stranded on a deserted island, which three people would you want with you (dead, alive or famous)? Jesus is a given!"

Would You Rather

Take turns going around the table and ask each person a "Would You Rather" question. Below are a few examples:

"Would you rather own a private jet or have the ability to teleport like in Star Trek?"

"Would you rather drive a really nice car or have a gorgeous home?"

"Would you rather speak to a huge crowd or hold a snake?"

Surprising Facts

Go around the room and have each person share one fact about them that would surprise the group. Below are a few examples:

"I have frog collection"

"I play the harp"

"I've swam with sharks"

I Have Never

Go around the room and have each person share something surprising that they have never done before. Examples:

"I have never been to the circus"

"I have never played paintball"

"I have never been outside of the US"

You can have everyone in the group who has had that experience raise their hands.

Who Has the Most?

Come up with a short list of questions (i.e.; the most: traffic tickets, children/grandchildren, cities lived in, pets, instruments they can play, pairs of shoes owned, etc.) and have people raise their hands to see who has the highest number in each category.

Favorite Holiday

Go around the room and have people say which holiday is their favorite and why.

Which Do You Prefer?

Have a list of two choices of different things. And have everyone say which one they prefer. (Examples: morning or evening, dogs or cats, introvert or extrovert, spaghetti or pizza, comedy or drama)

Birthday Pampering Favorite:

What are your first & second choices if you could pick any way to be pampered on your birthday?

Examples: Breakfast in bed, sleeping in, dinner, mani-pedi, or massage…

Personal Hero

Go around the room and have everyone say who their personal hero is and why.

Tips for Ministering to Needier Individuals

There are times when individuals will require more ministry than they can get in the small group setting. Often, they will look to you to minister and/or direct them to the ministry they need. Keep the following in mind:

- It is not only OK, but healthy to let people know you don't have all the answers.
- You are not the Source. Your job is to constantly point them to Christ.
- Remember, you are NOT responsible FOR, but only responsible TO love and honor people. Be very clear what loving and honoring looks like. If it feels heavy (and not "presence of Lord weighty"), you are probably taking on responsibility that is not yours. Review what responsible TO and FOR is on pp. 13-15 as needed.
- If there you have a co-leader or a more spiritually mature member of your group, ask if they can stay to help pray for a needier member.
- As you pray/minister with people:

    ❐ Set your affection on Christ.
    ❐ Take the time to center yourself mentally/emotionally smack dab in the middle of the Trinity.

    ❖ You are already seated in heavenly places (Eph. 2:6).
    ❖ Christ is in you (Col. 1:27).
    ❖ You are in Christ (Col. 2:10).

    ❐ Thank Him for these realities.
    ❐ Pray from the reality that everything the human race needs has already been provided for through the finished work of the cross (Rom 8:32).

- ☐ Thank Him for that reality (you don't need to beg God for what was His idea and passion in the first place).
- ☐ Thank Him for loving this son/daughter so much that He couldn't help Himself from sacrificing Himself to reconcile them back to Him.
- ☐ Thank God for giving you authority to trample on serpents and scorpions and over all the power of the enemy and nothing by any means shall harm you (Luke 10:19).
- ☐ Take authority over everything that has exalted itself against the knowledge of God and what He sacrificed for in Jesus's name. Note: salvation includes everything for man's highest good - body, soul, spirit, finances, relationships...and it is not dependent on our performance (Eph. 2:8-9).
- ☐ Thank Holy Spirit for backing up His word and His coming out your mouth.
- ☐ Thank Him for releasing angels assigned to minister to this heir of salvation (Heb. 1:14).
- ☐ If there are observable symptoms, ask if they have improved, and rejoice if there is improvement.
- ☐ If there is no improvement or they have gotten worse, thank Jesus for His answers, and for your authority in Him. Thank Him that He is so huge and had the answers in motion before the problem ever presented itself. Thank Him that He is the name above all names and that everything must bow to His name. Spend some time with this as you refocus and help the person refocus on Christ (Rev. 13:8; Phil. 2:8-9).
- ☐ As you get refocused, pray again for the symptoms and thank God for His majesty here - in Jesus's name - Amen.

- Even as you should pray for them, consider setting them up with a prayer partner, or partners, from the group.
- If at any time you feel over your head, seek pastoral help.
- If demonic manifestations happen (you'll know because they're just creepy), take your place in Christ mentally and command them to silence and back off in Jesus's name! YOU are the one in authority! Get back

up with security or 911 if you need. Do not try to cast them out alone unless you are experienced. This needs specific experienced ministry that is not in the scope of this course. Refer to pp. 32-34 where I talk about this in detail.
- Refer people who are in crisis, emotionally/spiritually wounded, or with demonic manifestations to pastoral staff. For other resources to help with this, see **ADDITIONAL RESOURCES.**

Additional Resources

For Inner Healing/Mind Renewal Help:

>The Safe Place Ministry
>http://inthesafeplace.com

Prayer Support (and Crisis Support as Needed):

>Andrew Wommack Ministries Prayer Line
>Mon. - Fri., 4:30 am - 9:30 pm MST
>719-635-1111, Option 1

*Don't forget appropriate naturopathic/medical support when there are probable brain chemistry issues. There is no condemnation to get natural help as well as prayer support. Whatever you do, do in faith.

Recommended Book Resources:

>*Boundaries: When to Say Yes, When to Say No, to Take Control of Your Life*
>   by Dr. Henry Cloud & Dr. John Townsend
>*Keep Your Love On* by Danny Silk
>*A Better Way to Pray* by Andrew Wommack
>*Believer's Authority* by Andrew Wommack
>*You've Already Got It!* by Andrew Wommack
>*Mystical Union* by John Crowder
>*Understanding the Whole Bible* by Jonathan Welton

Please Note: Imprint is not a church entity and does not have a hotline, prayer center or resources to provide crisis intervention or intensive individual counseling.

ABOUT THE AUTHOR

As an MD in residency, Catherine's life was radically transformed when she encountered the real Jesus, who walked her out of years of heavy bondage. In the process, He birthed a deep compassion in her to reach out to others with the love and power of a wildly passionate God who heals, transforms, restores the broken, oppressed and infirm, and releases them into powerful destinies. After 4 years practicing as a board certified Internist, she retired from medicine to raise her children and wholeheartedly pursue God's call on her life.

By divine connection, she met and served under Apostle Schlyce Jimenez in numerous capacities including prayer, healing, prophetic coaching, wholeness coaching, training, teaching, preaching and equipping.

Catherine was ordained as an Apostle and Prophet in February of 2015. Catherine is an anointed author and speaker. Her prophetic voice is acutely accurate in speaking forth vision, direction, confirmation, and practical strategic insight into individuals, leaders, and organizations around the globe.

In 2016, she founded Imprint, LLC, dedicated to restoring wholeness, revealing identity, and releasing destiny through the unveiling of God's imprint of love uniquely expressed in every person. In 2017, she released her first book, *Marked by Love*, which takes the reader on a wild encounter with God as Love to discover their true identity, through the lens of the imprint placed upon every person by God. Because of the book's wonderful reception, she followed up with a *Marked by Love* online course, workbook, leaders' guide, and *Rare and Beautiful Treasures* mini-book, with more books to come. She is a sought-out speaker and coach and resides with her husband and 3 powerhouse children in Colorado. For more information about Catherine Toon and Imprint, visit www.catherinetoon.com.

CONNECT:

![catherinetoon.com website banner – Author | Prophetic Speaker | Coach – Marked to Make Your Mark]

info@catherinetoon.com
markedbylovebook.com

Receive weekly videos direct to your inbox.

Sign up @ catherinetoon.com

FOLLOW:

Subscribe for fresh daily & weekly inspiration!

- **f** @CatherineToonMD
- **Instagram** catherinetoon
- **Twitter** @CatherineToonMD
- **YouTube** Catherine Toon, MD
- **LinkedIn** Catherine Toon

REQUEST:

To request Catherine for speaking engagements:

info@catherinetoon.com

OR – Visit: catherinetoon.com/Request

MARKED BY LOVE

ONLINE COURSE

—

Experience God in ways you never thought possible.

Are you tired of feeling stuck in the guilt trap, leaving you confused and disconnected from God? Imagine being secure and connected in your relationship with God, in a way that creates peace and wholeness in every area of your life.

What if you could experience God – anytime, anyplace, in any situation? What if you knew how to hear His voice all the time? How would that impact your life, your relationships, and your future? Marked by Love is an experiential course that will take you on a journey into the heart of Love. This course will touch the depths of your soul and you will experience Him in ways that you never thought possible.

For more information, go to: mbl.catherinetoon.com/info

OTHER PRODUCTS
BY CATHERINE

Marked by Love Book

Love is not only a powerful emotion, but a Person. This book provides an in-depth exploration of Love. Catherine will lead you to intimately encounter God as Love throughout the book with her 'Love Encounter Break' exercises. In doing so, you will begin to unveil the way He has uniquely and exquisitely created and marked you. As you connect with who you truly are, you will be empowered to make your unique mark on a world that is starving for Love.

"This beautiful volume…encourages you in your identity as created in the image of God… bolstering you in the depth of His sweet and tangible presence!" – **John Crowder,** Sons of Thunder Ministries and Publications

"You will feel whisked away into this giddy, spunky, irrational romance with her God of Love. Then, you will turn the page and find yourself crying as she drops a truth-bomb that hits your soul like a wrecking ball." – **Karen Welton,** Welton Academy

Marked by Love Workbook

Are you tired of hearing about the love of God, only to find that it doesn't feel real? Love is our deepest emotional and spiritual need and Love is a

Person. God is Love. Without Him as the Source of Love, we shrivel up, emotionally, spiritually, and physically. We limp through life. We have no idea who we really are, or the ultimate reason we are on the planet. This workbook compliments the acclaimed *Marked by Love* book and provides a Holy Spirit-guided adventure into experiencing the Person of Love. Catherine will lead you into intimate encounters with Love, and you will begin to unveil the exquisite ways that you have been created and marked by God. As you connect with who you truly are, you will be empowered to make your unique mark on a world that is starving for Love.

Rare & Beautiful Treasures Mini-Book

KEYS TO MOVE FROM BROKENNESS TO BEAUTY

The enemy of our souls has been defeated at the cross, but the kingdom of darkness has gotten a lot of mileage in a fallen world. But God is the One Who truly bring beauty for ashes. He does not gloss over the ugly, but honors you and honors your heart. Love truly is the Answer, because Love is a Person. God is Love, and Love never fails. He has specific answers for you. In her book, Catherine will help you with practical insights and keys to:

- Move from heartbreak to desires FULFILLED
- Encounter God's true goodness towards you
- Become CONFIDENT that you will experience transformation in your situation
- FEEL SAFE with God, and experience all the treasures He has for your life
- Find out how good God really is, so you can receive everything you are looking for
- See God TRANSFORM the broken and ugly into something overwhelmingly powerful and strikingly beautiful

So, buckle up your seatbelts. It's time to encounter God. It's time to encounter the One Who triumphed so that YOU can triumph! It's time to see the beauty of His treasures!

STAY TOONED...

Catherine's next book is coming:
Payback God's Way!
(release date TBD)

www.ingramcontent.com/pod-product-compliance
Lightning Source LLC
Chambersburg PA
CBHW080550170426
43195CB00016B/2742